Mid-Lands

Robert Murray Davis

MID-LANDS

A Family Album

The University of Georgia Press

Athens and London

*The publication of this book is supported
by a grant from the National Endowment
for the Arts, a federal agency.*

© 1992 by Robert Murray Davis
All rights reserved
Published by the University of Georgia Press
Athens, Georgia 30602
Designed by Louise M. Jones
Set in 10/14 Linotype Walbaum
   by Tseng Information Systems, Inc.
Printed and bound by Thomson-Shore, Inc.
The paper in this book meets the guidelines for
permanence and durability of the Committee on
Production Guidelines for Book Longevity of the
Council on Library Resources.

Printed in the United States of America

96 95 94 93 92   C   5 4 3 2 1

Library of Congress Cataloging in Publication Data
Davis, Robert Murray.
Mid-lands : a family album / by Robert Murray Davis.
p.   cm.
ISBN 0-8203-1392-0 (alk. paper)
1. Boonville (Mo.)—Social life and customs.   I. Title.
F474.B7D38   1992   977.8'51–dc20

                                   91-15039
                                        CIP

British Library Cataloging in Publication Data available

For all the Davises and Murrays, who got me this far;

for Megan, Jennifer, and John, who continue;

for Sarah, who goes with me

Contents

Mid-Lands

A Kind of Beginning

In 1987 I went back to Boonville, Missouri, where I grew up, to stay with my father while he recuperated from an operation. It went worse than expected, and my brother and sister and I, spelled occasionally by their children, spent a lot of time in the intensive care ward of the big hospital in Columbia, twenty miles to the east.

I was once accused of being a stoic, and at the time I wondered, in contrast to what? I was at least four hundred miles and easily ten years from my usual support systems. That's a psychobabble way of saying that I no longer knew anyone in Boonville not directly involved with Dad and that I didn't have my usual work or even a routine to distract me from the figure lying there with tubes and wires running from his body while I sat useless, the wrong kind of doctor when even the right kind could offer no real hope. In my youth, I had wanted to be bigger and stronger than Dad, and now I was. I had wanted to be myself rather than his son, and pretty soon I wouldn't have any choice. I had wanted to get away from Boonville, and I had gone farther than any of my widely extended family. And here I was.

When my daughter came into town to see her grandfather, I realized that her visit did a lot more for me than for Dad because it gave me a different kind of anchor. Not so much at the hospital, because I could see that she had no way of knowing how Dad and I had finally arrived at a way to communicate after more than fifty years of trial, error, and apparent indifference. But under the big walnut trees in Dad's yard and in other familiar territory in Boonville, it was easier to relax with her there.

One afternoon she asked if we could go to see the family plot in the cemetery, not the one across the street, but the Catholic cemetery a little way down the road, overlooking the prison. Since we are fairly recent arrivals in Boonville, having moved here only fifty years ago, our family plot isn't large: the graves of my maternal grandparents and uncle and my mother, with a spot for Dad next to her, his name and date of birth already on the stone.

My daughter knew these people only through family stories and a few photographs, and her real reason for the visit was to adjust to the idea that Grandpa was going to fill that empty space. She has always been a remorselessly logical child, so I wasn't really surprised, only a little taken aback, when, on the drive back, she asked, "Where would you like to be buried?"

I said that I would prefer to avoid it altogether, if possible, but she wasn't having any of that. I said that I had never really thought about it. Clearly I was going to have to think about it. "Well," I said finally, "I've always believed in research. Maybe I should leave my body to the medical school."

"What do you want us to do with the ashes when they finish?" (Jesus, you want your kids to be sensible, but even that can be carried too far.) "Do you want to be buried next to your mother?" I couldn't explain that my relationship to my mother got more complicated as I grew more independent and that it was hard to see it clearly because she had died more than twenty years ago. So I just said, "Not especially. Anyway, the point of a grave is so people can come and visit it, and you'll probably never come back to Boonville. When your grandpa dies, I probably won't come as often myself, and I only come about once a year now."

"Do you want to be buried in Norman?" I've lived in Oklahoma longer than I've lived anywhere, raised a family there, had a career there.

"I don't feel that Norman is home either. I remember your mother saying that she doesn't want a headstone, but she apparently does want to be buried. I guess I want a headstone but I don't care if I'm buried or not. Maybe you and your brother should decide between you. But make it cheap and convenient."

I don't know if that satisfied her, but at least it shut her up. When you've been a parent, you learn the trick of shifting responsibility, and sometimes you can get away with it.

But a day or so later she came back with another question: "How do you feel about grandchildren?"

The fact that, at twenty-three, she had to raise the question should have told her something, but then she didn't have my perspective. So I said a lot of wise father stuff. I had no qualms about being a grand-father, some of my best friends being grandmothers. I hoped that she would make decisions on the basis of her own desires and needs.

Her mother had surprised herself, our daughter said, by wanting grandchildren. The question, "Why do you feel differently?" seemed to be implied. Anyway, I answered it. "I feel about being a grandfather the way I feel about being buried. It just won't mean the same thing it used to. You and your brother won't be able to visit my grave. And I can't be a grandfather in the way my grandfather was to me. I can't even be a grandfather in the way yours was to you. For one thing, I won't have a place for the grandkids to come to. Besides, the way that my life has gone for the last ten years, I'm not likely to stay in one place that long."

Thank God they finally reach the age when they realize that no answer is as good an answer as they are going to get. Or at least they learn to live with it.

But I guess I didn't. Her questions stayed in my mind when, six months later in a raw, wet February, the family gathered for Dad's funeral. Technically, I was now head of the family—in fact, the oldest male in the extended family. It beats, as they say, the alternative, but it is a great relief not to have to act like a patriarch. All the immediate decisions had to be reached without me, and on the advice of lawyers, who pointed out the practical and legal complications of getting my signature on various documents, the long-range decisions were, with my approval, out of my hands. My siblings and I are partners rather than heirs in the usual sense because of the very sensible terms of Dad's will.

In my generation of the family, I am the odd one. My brother and sister still live in Boonville, my sister in the family home we moved into not long after World War II. Like Mom, my sister goes to work in an office. But the office is fifty miles away, and she manages the whole operation, not just the office. My brother does a little of this and that, here and there, in some of the same ways that Dad used to do them.

But in broader terms, I am far from the minority. Their kids are more like mine, in fact like me, than like their parents. One is in Germany; one is on her way there, though she wants to work in Japan. One is in St. Louis on her way to New Zealand. One, just back from six months in Peru, is on her way to the West Coast to interview for a job. At this point, my two nephews are the only members of that generation now living in Boonville. One took over his father's business. The other is living in the little house that his great-grandfather converted from a carriage shed, across the back yard from the big one, trying like his uncles to figure out what he wants to do when he grows up.

In broader terms still, I am solidly in the majority. The world I grew up in, between the end of the Second World War and the early fifties, I shared not just with my generation but with almost everybody born after 1900 and before 1945. They don't have to have come from a small town in the Midwest, though it would certainly help, because the world we inhabited was as much a mental construct as a physical place. And not even the most meticulous physical reconstruction can give the flavor of that time and place.

The title, *Mid-Lands*, refers to physical and psychic geography. Boonville, Missouri, isn't in the exact middle of the country, though close enough, but it was the center of my world. And that world, like all of them, was in the middle of a change that we couldn't see or begin to imagine.

This book isn't a memoir, though it has more personal materials than I planned. It isn't a social history, for I haven't done any research except to look at a map to refresh my memory and to read Robert L. Dyer's beautifully done *Boonville: An Illustrated History* to correct spellings and obvious anachronisms. Instead, it is like a series of photographs with annotations in a family album assembled so that my children can learn something about where I came from.

You may have noticed that old photographs of any family seem pretty generic. Sometimes the people are awkward, ridiculous, or stiff. Sometimes they are obviously trying to be funny but to us just look embarrassing. Were our predecessors really like that? Well, yes—the evidence is there. And no, because they didn't know that they were sitting or standing for a historical document. All we can see is what they looked like when they were standing still, mostly with their Sunday clothes and faces on. I can't pretend to tell you everything that they were thinking, but I do know something about it, and I think it is important to remember, partly because that is what my family does.

I did feel a little sheepish about recalling the sleepy Midwestern American forties as I was making notes in the fall of 1989, eighteen miles from the Romanian border, while the geopolitical map of Europe was re-bending itself into some very curious shapes. Hungary has history in ways that Americans cannot even imagine, and friends roughly my age have faced physical and moral challenges that make, or ought to make, me ashamed to grumble about anything in my life.

So I've tried not to grumble, less out of shame than from a sense that we don't need another book about a sensitive, misunderstood adolescent in a small town. At the same time, I refuse to believe that my experiences and those of my contemporaries are meaningless or irrelevant.

Revisionist American historians, including novelists and filmmakers, think that the social and political values of the early cold war period were escapist or paranoid and helped lead the country into the Vietnam War. Reactionary columnists and voters look back to the period as one of order and tranquility, when society was stable and the future unthreatening. Both sides could probably use these pages to support their views. But I am trying to tell how it was, or how I remember it. Or perhaps give shape to what I can remember from a past a lot of us shared.

Family and Others

Because young people lack experience from which to generalize and empathy with which to put themselves in others' places, they tend to believe that everybody else is different from them and probably from one another. In middle age, having acquired a great deal of experience and lost much of the surprise at idiosyncratic behavior and emotions, we tend to believe that everyone is essentially the same. Neither group is exactly wrong, but the truth of each side is easier to acknowledge than to apply. It is hard for me to apply it to myself and even harder to apply it to the Davis family—most of whom would energetically deny that they were the least bit like anyone except each other.

The difficulty, as I gradually became aware, was that while I knew I wasn't like anyone else, I was not at all sure that I could rise to the challenge and responsibility of being a real Davis. For one thing, as various family members and friends reminded one another over my head as far back as I can remember, I didn't look like a Davis. I had my father's cheekbones and dark complexion, but the forehead was a little too high, the nose a little too long, the build a little too thin and nervous, and the general attitude a little too withdrawn. The curly hair was just plain weird, and my relatives strained their memories to account for it. As the oldest and for five years the only child, I was given the impression that somehow I had failed, so it was not only tragic not to be like my father, it was socially irresponsible.

It is hard to explain why this bothered me so much. Like most young boys, I saw my father as so powerful, mysterious, and remote that I couldn't imagine ever becoming like him. Besides, I couldn't imagine any other model. Dad looked very unlike the fair, stocky, Germanic, and rather phlegmatic people in Boonville. At six feet, he was tall for his generation, and from the ground up he was lean all the way to the big chest and shoulders. He was a very good-looking man. Even as a boy he was sturdy, if short, and I envied my friend Ronnie Bledsoe not only because he seemed brave and sure of himself but because, according to my mother, he resembled my father. In his teens, Dad grew tall and lean. A photograph from the late 1920s shows him trying on the Rudolph Valentino look, hair slicked down, eyes lustrous and brooding under heavy brows, but by the time I have any clear memory of him, the lounge lizard look had been replaced by something more rugged and outdoorsy, perhaps Clark Gable in an adventure movie.

Dad was nowhere near as ebullient as Gable, and sometimes he could be as silent as Valentino. Though for much of life he bought and sold things to make a living, he didn't seem to talk any more than absolutely necessary. And he moved, not slowly, but with economy and deliberation. Grown-ups could joke with him, and his only response would be a sideways grin or a frown, but as far as I could tell, grown-ups were as aware as I that he was nobody to mess with. Everybody seemed to mess with me with impunity, at least until I was driven into a berserker's rage. So I was letting down the family by being passive or losing control as well as by my looks.

In fact, I looked something like my mother's side of the family, the Murrays, but that didn't seem much consolation. It was true, or seemed to me, that Mom was taller, darker, livelier, prettier, and moved more quickly and gracefully than the mothers of my contemporaries, but very few boys want to look like their mothers. Mom smoked cigarettes, which was still pretty daring for a woman in 1939, and would not refuse a drink. She claimed that she was almost twenty-five (after Prohibition ended) before she knew that it was possible to drink Dr. Pepper straight. In other ways, she seemed the antithesis of my father. If she didn't talk all the time, she talked a great deal. He seemed to choose his words very carefully, and though he could move very quickly, for the most part his movements were equally deliberate. When they clashed, she would get louder, he more silent. Only once did I hear of a physical confrontation. Dad rarely lost his temper, but when he did he was not just formidable (he was that normally) but frightening. Once my brother angered him and was sent to the basement for a whipping. Afraid that John would be hurt, Mom planted herself in front of Dad. He picked her up and put her to one side. "But," as she told the story later, "he didn't spank Johnny!"

(When Johnny had grown taller than Dad or I, one night at supper Mom choked on a piece of meat. This was before the Heimlich maneuver had been devised, and in desperation John picked her up, turned her upside down, and shook her. He dislodged the meat and also cracked one of her ribs. She seemed rather proud of his strength though rueful about the result.)

When I was still too young to be aware of the complexities of this or any other adult relationship, Dad seemed omnipotent, Mom omniscient. In one of my first memories of her, from the time I was two or three, I asked her to come from the other room to look at something I was doing, and she replied that she could see. It did not occur to me that she couldn't.

When we came to Boonville, she was not quite thirty and pregnant with my brother John, but this didn't seem to slow her down. Her hands moved as quickly as her mind and tongue. She loved to see new things. The MKT railroad bridge, which raised in the middle to let riverboats through, fascinated her, and when she heard a whistle, she would hustle me into the car and head for the riverbank to watch it. When she wasn't doing something, she was commenting, drawing on a large collection of taglines, some of them stock and some—"He had no more idea how to do it than a fuzzy bug" or "She didn't say 'Hello,' 'Kiss my foot,' or 'Go to hell,'"—peculiar to her, and the last pretty daring in her place and time. Even better, she was telling stories about her girlhood and early married life that on the one hand entertained me and on the other hand depressed me because I couldn't live up to her past any more than I could to my father's present.

According to Mom—and I never caught her in a flat-out lie or even much of an exaggeration—she was more enterprising than her brother Bob, a year older. She claimed to have ridden horses that he wouldn't even get on, displaying as evidence her left arm, shorter than the right after three breaks (to only one on the right). She claimed to have been as good a dancer, swimmer, and skater as Dad. I could believe it of her, but it seemed impossible that Dad could have been so frivolous. The only thing that didn't seem to fit with her character was a full complement of superstitions. Some were pious reflexes such as throwing spilt salt over the left shoulder and putting on the right shoe first. Fear of a black cat crossing her path was so deep that she would drive blocks out of her way to avoid one. And though she wasn't afraid of any horse or even Dad, she was the only person I have actually seen jump onto a chair when she saw a mouse.

She gave the impression of being very active, but for most of the years I knew her, she did no physical exercise (as a young man I teased her that she had never walked lengthwise on a sidewalk in Boonville). But she could still do the Charleston when it was briefly revived in the late 1940s. And once, when she was well past forty and my brother and

I started an impromptu contest to see who could kick the top of the doorframe leading into the kitchen, she walked over and, left foot on the floor, hit it with the right in one try.

Unlike the stereotyped mother of the period, she was intensely competitive. Her strongest memory of school was being unjustly marked wrong for putting three loops in an "m," spoiling her otherwise perfect lifetime spelling record. She asserted, not aggressively but as a matter of indisputable fact, that she was a better driver than anyone else who ever sat behind a wheel. During the Second World War, R. D. Patrick, an auctioneer and cattle trader, needed a bull transported to Texas and could not find a spare man to drive the truck. Mom offered to do it. When she was told she obviously couldn't because she was a woman, she raised such hell that everybody caved in, and, with R.D.'s wife for company, she made the trip both ways. (She had never seen cotton fields, and she stopped to pull up a stalk as a souvenir.) The most frustrated I ever saw her was when she attempted to drive a pickup that had a four-speed transmission no one had told her about. She kept putting the stick shift where reverse ought to be, and the truck would inch closer to the side of the building against which it was parked. She finally discovered—or, worse, had to ask—that reverse was not top left but somewhere else. She acted as if the laws of nature had been suspended just to embarrass her.

Mom seemed to operate on the principle that the real duty of people was not to be right but to be interesting, and she was the first storyteller I encountered in the family. In most, as seemed only natural, she was the heroine, and as she got older, the stories got more complicated and dramatic. There was the story about the young man who parked the car in a dark lane and got fresh with her. She slapped him upside the head, and when he got out of the car to show his indignation, she drove off and left him to walk home.

The story of how she first dated my father was even more complex.

Invited to a dance by a boy she found unsuitable, she told him that she already had a date. He spread the word, and no one else called her. The night of the dance she was sitting at a soda fountain, feeling sorry for herself. In walked Dad. Why wasn't she at the dance? She replied that she didn't have a date, so he asked her. She admitted to being a little disconcerted. He was obviously attractive and was known as a good dancer. But he also had a reputation for being rather wild. He had worked in a front for a bootlegging operation. He had left high school (with her brother) to go to work in the oil fields, a roughneck by reputation as well as occupation. But she did want to go to that dance.

Later, when he raised the question of marriage, she insisted that she would never marry a man without a high school diploma, so, several years older than his classmates, he went back to Arkansas City High School and gained an honorable place in the yearbook, where, in his copy, a very handsome girl signed her photo, "To Bubs, a real hunk of man."

Bubs was my father's childhood nickname—in fact, my Wichita cousins didn't know that his real name was (as he spelled it) Mathew— and Mom's was Bibs, presumably short for Elizabeth. Individually they sound cute, and in combination they sound nauseating, but the names made me realize that my parents had not always been Mom and Dad. Mom had been to a lot of parties, parts of which she would describe. Her brother—sounding very unlike my reserved Uncle Bob— had gone off to rotten egg the school principal's house but wound up with egg all over his sweater. He and my father were silent to their graves about who pushed the streetcar down the Summit Street hill into the irrigation canal. Dad wouldn't talk about the faint scar on his left cheek which he had received in a fight over a girl with a Mexican much bigger than he. Once Bubs had hit his older brother Pug (as we knew Uncle Gough) in the face with a plate of butter during an argument at dinner and was chased down the road and up a tree.

Sometimes it seemed as though the real point of living was not to be strong or brave or successful but to have stories told about you. So in addition to feeling little and weak and timid, I was afraid that I was boring.

It was bad enough not being able to provide material for anecdotes, but when I began to hear stories from and about my father's side of the family, I came to realize that I was at the tail end of a whole chronicle about people I didn't look like and couldn't possibly live up to.

The underlying theme of every story was that Davises were sturdy, energetic, resourceful, direct, and optimistic, often in courageous or bullheaded defiance of the facts. Furthermore, they had been going on an unimaginably long time, past the Civil War (blending Connecticut Yankees and Virginia Confederates), past the Revolution, past the reign of Elizabeth, somehow connected to Thomas of Woodstock, son of Edward III, the chain extending as my grandmother and aunts went deeper and wider into genealogy. They had been disguised under names like Cary, Gough, Bustin, Chaffee, and Whitaker until Grandma Davis, born a Bustin, left widowed by a Sweeney, took to husband Dolphin Chaffee Davis and the true family banner could be unfurled.

The real story was found not in the genealogical charts but in the family saga of which my aunt Cary has been custodian and narrator, in a series of discontinuous, synchronic, and gradually expanding anecdotes, for as long as I can remember. The history didn't have to be glorious—sometimes I got the impression that the more discreditable it was, the better—but it did have to be interesting. Since the family had a tradition of posthumous children dating back at least to 1595, when the Cambridge theologian William Whitaker (Protestant: another Davis family tradition) left a widow pregnant with our ancestor Jabez (who built the first rail fence in the Jamestown colony), many of the stories dealt with bad things happening to men. A Confederate ancestor, home on leave, went hunting, and treed a critter. Cary says it was a raccoon, but possum sounds more Confederate. Unwisely, he stood underneath and was struck and killed when another hunter broke the branch to dislodge the prey. Cary discovered in the Mormon records in Salt Lake City a Connecticut woman who in the eighteenth century avoided prosecution for counterfeiting by turning in her brother on the same charge. Cary was delighted with the woman's resourcefulness and much disappointed to find that we descended not from her but from the brother. She was only a little disconcerted when I pointed out that her son had, as a boy, followed in the family tradition by melting down slugs to the size of nickels and gained the attention of the FBI. That too was a good story.

Men had not fared much better in the twentieth century. Grandma Davis's second husband was attracted by the cooking in her mother's boarding house in Birmingham, Alabama, and discovered only after the wedding that the black cook rather than Grandma was responsible for it. So he moved the family to Kansas, fell off a freight car, got a small disability pension, and spent the rest of his days baking the baby chicks in an incubator, bungling other simple chores, and reading Dickens and Bulwer-Lytton novels in the attic. Anyway, this was the version told by Cary.

The Davises were definitely matriarchal. Grandma Davis had died before I was old enough to remember her, but Cary's accounts of her made her seem more vivid than my living grandmother. Judging from Cary's stories, "Mama" was an energetic pursuer of schemes that never quite worked. If she impressed Cary, she must have been a real force. The only information Dad conveyed was that his mother was short and that even after her hands were crippled with arthritis, she would play "Listen to the Mockingbird" for him on the piano. He never talked about his father at all.

Grandma Davis may have dominated her household, but she didn't overshadow her daughters. Nanelou Sweeney, born of her first marriage, was the first family member to graduate from college in living memory. Technically, according to the stereotype of the time, she was an old maid schoolteacher, but she was a large, powerful woman of surprisingly varied tastes, as indicated by her choice of rather raffish Christmas and birthday books like *Suds in Your Eye* and a very lightly expurgated *Gulliver's Travels*. I learned to write letters by thanking her for these and other gifts. Cary, the oldest surviving child from the second marriage, has outlived both of her children and several grandchildren and finds it hard to remember that she is over ninety. The last time I saw her she was trying to climb on an upturned five-gallon can to clamber in the window of a locked house.

My father seemed to me utterly independent and invincible, but in fact he was the baby of the family. He and his surviving brother were the youngest in the family by eight to ten years and their nicknames (Bubs for Mathew, Pug for Gough) indicated their lack of status. They had in effect three mothers, Grandma, Nanelou, and Cary.

Dad also played a subordinate role in the family saga. The story repeated most often deals with his attempt to confront Cary. About 1923, when he was fifteen, he traveled from Arkansas City, Kansas, to visit Cary in Albuquerque, New Mexico. They had driven south to El Paso, and on the way back were near what is now called Truth or Consequences, fairly desolate even now and far more so then. He was annoying Cary, who was much aware of her superior status as an older sister and young married woman, by smoking a cigarette, by the way he drove, and finally by chewing a quid of tobacco. She said he couldn't continue to drive if he chewed tobacco, so he stopped the car, got out, and walked around to the passenger side. Down the road he found new ways to annoy her, and finally she told him to shape up or get out. "Stop the car," he said, and got out in the middle of nowhere, thinking to call her bluff. She drove off. "I cried all the way back to Albuquerque," she told my children a half-century later, "but I didn't turn around."

Dad could see a town in the distance, so he trudged across the desert, slept on a roof ("Damn near froze to death!"), and in the morning found a good samaritan who bought him breakfast. He telegraphed his brother-in-law for carfare back to Albuquerque, and even then he avoided Cary for a day or two. Telling the story years later, he showed not resentment at being left behind but respect for someone even more stubborn than he.

Why he would confront Cary when he had lost an earlier contest of wills with a lesser mortal was a tribute to his own stubbornness. About 1920, having earned some money for carfare in prize fights against other teenagers, he visited Cary in the White Mountains of northern Arizona. Allowed to go with a young Mexican who was packing supplies to a work crew, he got into an argument with his guide about something that nobody seemed to remember and had to wander around until he located a pack burro that led him out. In later years he was hard to budge for trips, and no wonder, I thought, since every time he went somewhere he got left.

My mother, who had never had to walk home from anywhere, regarded the Davis mystique with the kind of skepticism she trained on almost all human activities and institutions except, from her father's side, the Republican party and, from her mother's side, the Catholic Church. Looking at what purported to be the family crest, topped by a stylized waterfowl, she translated the Latin motto as "The goose hangs high." She did like the stories, however, and I think that she appreciated the contrast that the Davises provided to both sides of her family on a number of counts—southerners from Alabama as opposed to Yankees from Evansville, Indiana; sons and daughters of various past wars as opposed to recent immigrants or agenealogical migrants; Protestants as opposed to Catholics; Democrats as opposed to Republicans; drivers of Chevrolets as opposed to Fords. Besides, Cary and Nanelou seemed to think of her as a Davis who had unaccountably been born with a different name.

I was closer to my mother than to my father for the first two decades of my life, partly because that is the way boys are raised and partly because, I came to realize, there was a lot of Murray in my character as well as my looks. I could also see, less and less dimly, that she too wanted to be like her father. Mom was by birth half Litschgi, christened Bertha after her mother. She suppressed that name, as much because it was her mother's as because it sounded odd, and in imagination she was all Murray, sprung from the brain of her father like Athena from that of Zeus. The Litschgis were the last of my ancestors to get off the boat, and her mother, of the first generation born in this country, spoke German at home and half of each day in the school she left after the eighth grade. One of the collateral members of the family was a priest, over eighty the one time I saw him, but on the whole the Litschgis were rather dim figures in her view and, though they were pleasant enough to me, in mine.

Grandma was a living illustration of the German motto for women: *Kirche, Kinder, Kuche.* Courted by a militant atheist (whose family is buried in a Catholic cemetery), she insisted on a church wedding and attended mass as often as possible until she went into a nursing home. After bearing my uncle Bob and my mother a year and a week apart, she had a tubal pregnancy that precluded further children. The last time I saw her, withdrawn into senility, she mentioned Oliver, the baby she had lost, as if he were still alive. She was a stunningly good cook in the old-fashioned, heavy cholesterol style. She worried about children climbing trees or getting run over by cars or bulls or getting wet or going hungry. She never learned to drive a car. I have an image of her sitting with her hands folded in her lap on the rare occasions when she wasn't darning or peeling something. Mom was determined not to follow in her mother's hausfrau footsteps, and as her housekeeping and culinary efforts demonstrated, she succeeded quite well.

Her father, Robert J. Murray, came from a large family of boys, but mythologically speaking, he had no origin. Except for a few tales about practical jokes on his brothers, he had no family history. I only met one of his brothers, Ells, who visited us once in Boonville. Grandpa scorned his six-cylinder Ford because "it wouldn't pull the hat off your head." Later Ells killed himself with a shotgun, first spreading newspapers over the bed so that he wouldn't make a mess. I got the impression that Grandpa thought this typically feeble.

For a long time, we were under the impression that the Murrays were Irish, though it was difficult to imagine that connection for a Republican atheist with no Irish patriotism. But according to my sister's genealogical research, his family was Scottish.

Grandpa didn't care enough even to talk about his background, which was very unusual for him because he would talk, convincingly or knowledgeably or entertainingly or all three, about almost anything in a rather high, penetrating voice. If he wasn't explaining something he was swearing at it. Like Mom, he had a collection of folk sayings, but his were even pithier: "He couldn't find his ass with both hands"; "It's raining like a cow pissing on a flat rock"; and a good many others I can't attribute to him because I have appropriated them. He read everything but poetry or fiction. He had had a wide variety of jobs: postman, grocer, politician, farmer, amateur veterinarian, aircraft worker, bicycle shop owner, traveling salesman. He had served in the National Guard unit in Evansville which had tried to break up a race riot. As a small child, I had so much faith in his ability that, according to family memory, my recurrent line about anything broken was, "Grandpa fix it."

The only stories he told were obvious and artful lies in the Mark Twain tradition, and every time he told them, like the one about my father abandoned in the mountains, they got longer, wilder, better, and less reproducible. The shortest one I can remember is about a famous liar passing a group of men lounging in front of a store. They ask him to stop and tell them a lie. "I haven't got time," he answers. "George Smith just fell off his roof and broke his leg, and I'm going for the doctor." Five minutes later George Smith walks down the street.

Although I spent far more time with Grandpa Murray during my high school years than I did with my father, it didn't occur to me to want to be like him. For one thing, he wasn't a very big man, probably about 5'8", and he had never been athletic. By the time I knew him, he was in his early sixties and seemed a little paunchy. He had very bad eyesight, a double truss, and hay fever which made him and everyone around him miserable. Not at all the heroic type.

Moreover, it seemed impossible to emulate him because I didn't know anyone remotely like him. Stories about him were far more exciting than anything in the Davis saga. If they are anywhere near true, and they seem to check out, he was indifferent to physical danger and legal consequence.

Over thirty, with two small children and spectacularly unfit for trench warfare, he volunteered unsuccessfully for active service on the day the United States entered the First World War. My mother told of driving with him, when she was a little girl, into a small town and seeing armed men running from the bank to a waiting car. Without hesitating, Grandpa pulled a gun from the glove compartment and drove in pursuit, firing left-handed at the robbers. Since he was nearsighted and right-handed, his aim was worse than his intentions.

Given more time for reflection, he compensated for his limitations. A year or so after the end of the 1919 flu epidemic, he was commissioner of Cowley County in southern Kansas when a cold spell severely reduced the pressure in the main natural gas pipeline running from Oklahoma to Wichita. In order to maintain service to the city, the gas company officials shut off the side-line to Arkansas City, the county seat, leaving the residents, who had vivid memories of the epidemic, without heat.

With no time or inclination to get an injunction, Grandpa loaded a pinch bar and a shotgun, more appropriate to a nearsighted man, and drove out to the pumping station. He backed off the attendant with the gun, broke the lock on the valve wheel with the bar, and turned on the gas. Then he told the attendant, "I'm going back to Ark City, and I'm sending out a man with a rifle. If that valve is closed, he has orders from me to kill you." I don't know if the rifleman ever came, but the attendant obviously believed Grandpa because the line stayed open. Grandpa almost got in a lot of trouble, my father told me, but in fact he didn't. His exploit got him a good deal of publicity and the nickname "Pinch-Bar Murray."

Later, before the Depression wiped out his investments and ate up his business holdings, he was Cowley County's representative in the Kansas state legislature. By the end of the Depression, keeping a grocery store in Florence, Missouri, a crossroads hamlet, he was elected state representative for Morgan County and helped, to his great satisfaction, discomfit the Prendergast machine in Kansas City and Harry Truman, whom he disliked intensely and whom he resembled not a little in native shrewdness and refusal to apologize for his regional background. He said that he liked to introduce outrageous bills just to see what would happen.

When the Second World War broke out, he did not run for reelection but moved back to Evansville to help build P-47 fighter planes, which he regarded as far superior to the P-51, just as he regarded Republicans as superior in design and execution to Democrats beyond any possibility of debate.

In fact, Grandpa didn't like to debate; he liked to argue. In debate each side gets a turn. One major difference between the Murrays and the Davises was that the Murrays were sure they were right and would not stop until the misguided opposition was converted or overwhelmed. The Davises were so sure that they were never wrong—"right" often seemed to be defined as anything a Davis chose to do—that they didn't even bother to argue with anyone unfortunate enough to be denied election. Once I overheard an in-law saying in exasperation to a sibling, "The trouble with you Davises is that you think you can do stuff better than anyone else." When I repeated the line to some cousins, their spouses exchanged significant looks. On the other hand, however clannishly the Davises saw themselves, they didn't seem to take themselves too seriously. The Murrays, which meant Grandpa and Mom, didn't seem to take anyone seriously.

Davises and Murrays did share a disinclination to be defined by a particular place. Davises were so confident and clannish that they assumed they belonged wherever they lit, or wherever they lit belonged to them. Murrays were gregarious enough to make themselves welcome just about anywhere. My contemporaries in Boonville had extended families, but only in numerical terms. It was a big move from Tipton to Boonville, roughly twenty miles. My family spread from Evansville to Albuquerque and varying spots between.

By the time I was ten, I had covered much of that space. My parents alone had lived in at least four places—three Kansas towns and a Missouri farm—during my first four years. In 1939, before I was five, they put me on a train from Missouri to Wichita, Kansas, where Nanelou met me and conveyed me to Albuquerque. There I got to know Cary's family and got to go to the Sandia Mountains where Nanelou served as counselor at a Girl Scout camp. It must have been 1943, before I was nine, when my parents put me on a bus to Evansville, with a change in St. Louis, to spend the summer with Grandpa and Grandma Murray. And there were more frequent visits with Uncle Bob (Robert J. Murray, Jr., who was less vivid than his father and sister and less handsome than my father) and Aunt Goldie in the village of Otterville, Missouri, in the southwestern corner of Cooper County.

I began to see that not all Davises were alike, that in fact being a Davis, or at least a live one, was a lot more complicated than the stories made it seem. Nanelou was large, confident and rather artistic. Cary was short, confident and as practical as a sledgehammer about real estate and everything else and seemed to know every Anglo and most Hispanics and Indians in New Mexico. Uncle Pug, whose antipathy for Dad was reciprocated with compound interest, was, according to the Missouri branch, pretentious (he had a big house and played opera records) and financially unreliable (an oil well promoter, he had twenty-one dry holes in a row). My father gambled in more conventional ways with cards (successfully) and dice (less so), and his sisters seemed as unable to account for his week-long drinking bouts after months of sobriety as for my curly hair. I couldn't explain his drinking either, and I began to see not only that I couldn't be like him but that I didn't even want to be. On the other hand, I sympathized increasingly with his desire to break loose from his everyday self.

Mom seemed comfortable enough with who she was; she just liked to go to new places. I shared that taste. In one of my earliest memories I am barely tall enough to see in a store window, and Mom swoops down and snatches me up with mixed annoyance and relief at having found her wandering child.

But I also resembled Dad in wanting to get away from my self or my circumstances. I was often unhappy in Boonville—physically small for my age with a big mouth, an unfortunate combination on the playground—and I found a way out in travel. The visits to Otterville were a little boring because there wasn't much to do and they weren't real trips. But longer journeys, especially unaccompanied, gave me the sense that I was doing something daring and unusual, even for a Davis. And there was family at the other end, far more tolerant, even supportive, of my idiosyncrasies than the citizens of Boonville.

I began to realize that it wasn't necessary to become a Davis; I just was a Davis. And to have stories told about me, I just had to live and act because Davises were by definition interesting. For instance, when I was perhaps three, my parents ran a restaurant in Arkansas City called the Silk Hat, and I thought that going there was a real treat. So when Nanelou took me to the Presbyterian church service with her, bored even then, I stood on the pew and declaimed, "Let's go to the Sick Cat and get a beer." Nanelou professed to be mortified, but she told the story with relish.

Fifty years after it happened, Cary tells a story from my visit in 1939. Involved in building the community center in Albuquerque's University Heights, she took me to the site for what she said was a picnic and put me to work at some minor task. Apparently I minded the work less than the misdirection, for she quoted me as saying, "I've heard of eating picnics and playing picnics, but I never heard of a digging picnic."

More in line with my father's tradition was the story of my trip to Evansville. When I got to St. Louis, I was pointed to a large bus with a sign reading "Indianapolis" on the front. Near it was a school bus painted red, white, and blue and probably called a victory bus, since that label was applied to everything conceivable during the war. Its sign said "Evansville," so I got aboard. We jolted across Illinois and reached Evansville an hour or more before the real bus. Nobody was at the station to meet me. I had my grandparents' phone number, but nobody answered. I had their address and some money, so I took a cab to 2856 Pennsylvania and sat on the porch steps confident that someone would turn up sooner or later, anxious only about being reimbursed. Before long my grandparents drove up. They had met the real bus, Grandma near panic because I wasn't on it. Grandpa asked pointed questions of the staff and realized what had happened. Grandma worried about it for years afterward, but the story—a real action, not just a one-liner—gave me new status in the family. Grandpa had material for another tall story and almost incidentally seemed proud of my resourcefulness in a solo performance.

That summer, Grandma often took me to the Evansville zoo. I remember best the monkey ship, rigged with several masts and numerous ropes and set in a broad pool. I could watch the monkeys' acrobatics and begging behavior for what seemed like hours. But most fascinating was a small monkey who, apparently tired of trying to compete for food, had learned to swim. He would dogpaddle out to a stake, seat himself on it, and gather in the peanuts tossed by his admirers. The older monkeys were furious. They would hang from ropes as close to the water as they dared, shake their fists, and shriek curses.

I admired that monkey. He had learned to do something difficult in order to go where no one else could go, and he obviously didn't give a damn what anyone else thought of him. If I could learn to do something different, perhaps I could get away from the situations and people that seemed oppressive. The difference between that monkey and me, I dimly realized even then, was that however strangely I acted or however far I went, my family would cheer me on. Grandpa Murray wouldn't even think it unusual. The Davises would see it as another good story. My parents would pretend to worry, but they would get over it.

Both sides of the family taught me to look at living as impromptu performance, ensemble on the Davis side, monologue on the Murray, in an unending picaresque that, no matter how frustrating or even disgraceful to the individual, brought pleasure to the family audience.

And the others? What others?

Perspectives

Boonville, Missouri, is only rarely celebrated in song and story. Chuck Berry lists it in a series of towns on the MKT (Missouri, Kansas, and Texas Railroad, or Katy) in "All Aboard." In Jack Kerouac's *On the Road*, Dean Moriarity points from the back of a bus crossing the Missouri River bridge to the Training School for Boys in Boonville where he once did time. But most people who know the name at all read it on the exit signs from the interstate. The only indications of urbanity on groomed banks rising twenty feet on either side of the twin slabs are standard intersection businesses—motels, truck stops, McDonalds. Otherwise, rural landscapes, indistinguishable from anything a hundred miles in either direction.

Fifty years ago the town was impossible to ignore because U.S. 40, the main artery that stretched from Baltimore to San Francisco, ran through it along Main Street, on the broad ridge between two valleys, south from the Missouri River bridgehead a dozen blocks before making a ninety degree angle west toward Kansas City by way of Golf Course Hill.

I still think of the highway running from east to west for reasons that are more social and economic than geographic because, even or especially to those who had never been there, the east was more important and intimidating than the west. But in fact, when my parents first saw

Boonville in 1939, they were coming from the west and saw, from the top of Golf Course Hill, Boonville spread out east-northeast below, the streets lined with trees. My mother said that this view made her want to live there. Dad was looking for a place with a pool hall for sale, and the one in Marshall hadn't been suitable.

Why he was looking for a pool hall in the first place or why we were moving from Kansas was never explained to me. Why Missouri is a little easier to reconstruct, since my mother's brother was raising chickens in Otterville and her father was running a store in Florence, Missouri, and serving in the state legislature. My brother John speculates that things had gotten too hot for Dad in Kansas. The liquor license for the multipurpose store Dad later opened was in Mom's name, and, knowing Dad's habit of playing everything close to the vest, John thought that Dad must have had a felony on his record. But since in the late 1960s he became a city councilman and later ran for county commissioner, either he didn't have a record or he had it expunged. Anyway, he found a pool hall for sale in the middle of downtown, and the family had found a home.

Golf Course Hill is still the best place from which to view the town. All the elm trees have gone, but there are plenty of others left to veil all but the largest buildings. The eye sweeps from the soft red brick and brighter roofs of Kemper Military School in the valley below straight across, in line of sight, to the pale stone of the Cooper County courthouse and the arches of the bridge across the invisible river.

If you had driven down the hill into town in 1946, the year I turned twelve, you would have noted only a few differences from what my parents first saw. The war had been over just about a year. To satisfy the lust for new cars, two dealerships had risen near the nine-hole, sand-green golf course—one of them the first Quonset-hut motif in town.

These were new, but down at the L onto Main Street clustered long-established businesses, including gas stations on three of the corners. Two blocks up the hill were three more gas stations; another block and two more; another and a large garage.

Downtown proper began across Locust Street from Laura Speed Elliott High School, whoever she was, and ran for five blocks, with block-deep businesses on either side and on Sixth Street, parallel to Main or Fifth.

The street names were and are generic: numbers for those running north and south, starting at the Katy tracks in the valley west of downtown. Mostly names of trees east and west until you come to Spring Street in the very heart of downtown and then Morgan (whoever he was) and High, along the bluff that ran precipitately down to Water Street, aptly named during the frequent floods on the Missouri, and a world never seen by tourists and seldom by most of the town's white population.

Drivers passing through would have seen nothing remarkable except the Lyric, a theater building unusually large for a town of 6,000, its brick columns painted white. The Casino, which showed Republic westerns and other B movies (and lower), was tucked into a block of buildings on the opposite side of the next block. Kemper State Bank, faintly neoclassical, and J.C. Penney's, both taller or at least more imposing than anything on their blocks, held the west corners of Main at Spring where the traffic light hadn't been installed yet. Toward the bridge on the east side of Main was Pete's Cafe, advertised with hundreds of white on red signs to the borders of flanking states as AIR CONDITIONED, with the red a little fresher where the AAA logo had been painted out. The courthouse at the corner of Main and High was noticeable because it was set back from the street, its lawn held back by retaining walls made of polished stone. But the Hotel Frederick, though large, would have to be ignored because the narrow entrance to the bridge demanded your attention, and by the time you reached the grain elevator rising past the bridge floor from the river side, you were busy trying to hold the car steady on a surface that seemed to squirm under the tires.

You would have seen a few chain stores—Penney's (the only store in town with a second floor, with little ceramic baskets on wires to carry your money upstairs to the cashier), Woolworth's, of course, Mattingly's, and the catalog store of what everyone called Monkey Wards. No franchises until the Dairy Queen, about 1949, and that seemed familiar because it was owned by the brother-in-law of my exact contemporary, Johnny McShane, whose father managed Penney's. Most of the stores were named after the town or region or, more commonly, for their owners: the drug stores—Phelps's (later Foster's), Long's, Miller's, Waldersheid's, Hirsch's; Pete's Cafe, for the tourist and local Sunday trade; Holt's Cafe, also the Greyhound bus station, which stayed open later than anywhere else in town and seemed raffish to those who didn't plan to go anywhere; Hirlinger's, where you could buy Hardy Boy books and baseball gloves as well as irrelevancies like stationery and office supplies, which smelled differently because of the leather and clean paper; Hirlinger's Confectionery, smelling of sugar, where the social elite of the (all-white) public high school sprawled in the dark-wooded booths, ignoring the marble-topped tables in the center; Victor's for men's clothes; Glover the Clothier; Brownsberger's.

To see any sign of industrial development, you would have had to drive west down the hill on Spring or Morgan. In this valley, where the Katy tracks ran south from the bridge that raised to allow riverboats through, stood the largest corncob pipe factory in the world (they had made a special model for General Douglas MacArthur) and a factory that made women's shoes, where a lot of poorish white people worked. Both were made of red brick and had more than one story, which seemed imposing. On the slope rising toward downtown some businesses dealt in agricultural products, and there were two hatcheries that smelled very odd indeed. There was an ice plant, though at some point—I had gotten too old to cadge chips of ice from the drivers—the delivery trucks with the heavy leather flap at the back had disappeared along with the metal-lined wooden iceboxes. By the late forties, the plant was doing a good business renting cold storage lockers to people who wanted to store up sides of beef. A few more industries, including a sand and gravel plant that drew its materials from the river bed, stood by the Missouri Pacific tracks that paralleled the river and the landing where a few riverboats could put in but never seemed to.

If you were a stranger and you wanted to stay the night in town, you had the choice of the Hotel Frederick, which had a view of the river and the bottom land across it, high ceilings, and a real lobby, or Baker's, a "family" hotel—friends of my family, in fact—a few doors west of Main on High Street, the lower and less fashionable end. Across the street, its back to the river, was the Commercial, a slightly seedy hotel which then was just old but is now considered to have historical significance. Down by the Katy tracks was a very seedy hotel and restaurant that nobody I knew ever went into. No motels. Across the river, in a seedy roadside strip of garages and small stores, was a row of rock tourist cabins. West of town was Big Bend, a restaurant, gas station, and row of wooden cabins that my parents—mostly Mom, since Dad worked on the Katy—ran during the war. And a couple of two-story nineteenth-century brick houses with turrets and sweeping porches on south Main advertised themselves as tourist homes, somewhat like bed and breakfast places but more obviously fallen on hard times.

Very little to tempt the traveler to leave Main. Very little attempt to do so, since the chamber of commerce would not for years discover the historical as well as financial value of the Indian mound at Harley Park and the view of the river from the scenic drive (Pecker's Point, male teenagers called it—it had a name—Harley Street—but I didn't know it until just now, when I looked it up) or the elegant brick houses on High Street east of the Hotel Frederick. Everyone knew that Frank James had been kept in the stone county jail, but this seemed only to prove how backward we were. A marker in front of the Lyric commemorated one of the Civil War battles, but the sites were not developed and that of the first battle in all Missouri, out near the Catholic (and only) hospital, could be discovered only by the determined antiquarian. I wasn't one and didn't know any. My Confederate ancestors came from a long way off, and most of the German immigrants had arrived in the area after the war and their descendants weren't interested in history anyway.

The closest thing to historic or military significance was Kemper Military School. The town boys called the cadets Squirrels, presumably after the grayish uniforms they wore, and resented them as rich delinquents who lusted (worse, successfully) after the girls of the town. Some local grownups resented the control, real or fancied, exercised by the management of Kemper over the economy of the town, and it was rumored that the Kemper hierarchy had blocked the building of a war plant near Boonville.

Still, the school offered some advantages. The campus was picturesque. During the summer my friends and I enjoyed riding our bicycles around the maze of drives and walks between the deserted and ivy-covered buildings. During the school year the cadet corps had a public parade on Sunday, and during the fall we could walk down the Katy tracks behind the stadium and sneak into the Kemper or Boonville High School football games. The only golf course, the only indoor swimming pool, the only running track, and the only tennis courts in town belonged to Kemper. We were constantly being told that Kemper was historic in the sense that it had been there a long time, but as far as we knew, the only famous person to attend Kemper was Will Rogers. He took the first opportunity to run away from Kemper and from Boonville; that made him popular with me.

On the other side of town, two hills away, you could look at poor delinquents, black as well as white, at the Missouri Training School for Boys, whose brick buildings and tree-lined streets, without bars or fences, looked like the campus of a downstart rural teacher's college. We had a lot more respect for the Training School boys than we did for the Squirrels. They wore shabbier uniforms and walked in looser and segregated formation, but they were connected to serious life in ways that, it seemed to us, the cadets were not.

It was easier to get a formal tour of those facilities, but except for the fully equipped print shop, which I wished I had access to, there was less to see than at Kemper. On the other hand, you could watch the boys march and play team sports all year round.

Between the two institutions you would see a lot of people who looked pretty much alike. The poor could be distinguished from the moderately well off, but the wealthy were harder to spot, partly because they were not very visible to young people and partly because money was not flaunted. In some cases, it was so fiercely hoarded that the technically rich looked very much like the poor. My grandfather said that one farmer was so tight that he had eighty-four cents and all the feathers off the eagle of the first dollar he had ever made. And there were a lot of hoarded feathers in Cooper County.

People who wore suits and didn't sweat were probably lawyers or bankers or haberdashery salesmen, and they did not spend much time on the streets where my contemporaries and I could see them. Only farmers wore jeans or overalls, and except for Saturdays, they didn't spend much time on the streets either. Women wore dresses and some wore hats even on weekdays. Even men wore hats, felt in the winter, straw in the summer. And they had brims all the way around; the baseball-style "gimme" cap did not come into vogue for another fifteen years or so.

You would see a few Negroes, as we called them when we were being polite, but far fewer than the actual percentage of the population except some men on Chestnut Street near the second-floor Blue Room Cafe, just over one of Kenny Esser's liquor stores, on the route between the Catholic school and Foster's Drug Store. You would rarely see a black and a white even speaking to each other unless the white spoke first, and that usually meant that he wanted something done.

Nobody looked foreign, though—no Asians or even Italians or Jews. Pete Christus, who owned the best-known restaurant in Boonville, was obviously Greek, but he had been in town so long that he was part of the background. That was the key—to be so familiar that everyone important, which meant grown-ups, knew you, including your oddities. No matter how claustrophobic the town came to seem to me, I realized that if you had any connections to speak of, the adult world tended to make allowances for you.

Space and Time

The world of every small town in the late 1940s was a good deal smaller than my children or even my nieces and nephews, who grew up in Boonville, can imagine. Most of us knew where we sat with reference to the rest of the state, country, and even world, and of course newspapers carried information about far-off places where we had been involved in war. The movies at the Casino and Lyric theaters offered backgrounds—mostly studio shots in those days—to go with names like London and Chicago, and grainy, washed-out black-and-white newsreels showed us a world that seemed crowded and threatening despite the hollow heartiness of the announcers. There was, of course, no television. In fact, Boonville had no radio station. Its daily newspaper, often four pages thin, carried social notes—baby showers, visitors from far-off points like Sedalia—from Speed and Lone Elm and other centers of civility and a little national and international news. There was a weekly newspaper, the *Cooper County Missourian*, which I didn't know about until I went to work for it, which didn't even have a teletype. For real news and contact with the outside world, people depended on the home-delivered *Kansas City Times* and *Star* or the *St. Louis Post-Dispatch*, which was harder to get because it came from half again as far away in linear space and from further than that in idea.

There weren't any physical barriers to keep you in town. Boonville was a hub for several highways, good ones by current standards. The wartime speed limit of thirty-five miles per hour had returned to Missouri's "reasonable and proper," which meant whatever you could get away with; and gasoline, tires, and new cars were once more available. Greyhound buses followed U.S. 40 right down Main Street. The Missouri Pacific passenger station was at the end of Second Street beside the river. But not many people I knew did leave.

Of those who did, the more cosmopolitan went to the very edges of the state: Kansas City, a hundred miles west, or, more exotically, to St. Louis, a hundred and fifty miles east, to shop or find amusement in outdoor musical theater or zoos or less clearly specified activities. Sports fans—that meant baseball—had to go to St. Louis to see major league baseball at the western edge of the two eight-team leagues, though I don't remember anyone admitting to seeing the Browns. Boonville was Cardinal country. You could walk down Main Street during the season and never miss a play on the Cardinal radio network because almost every business had the radio on and almost all doors were open. A trip to either city was a real expedition: you got up very early and came back very late. Nobody I knew stayed overnight.

East and west, Kansas City and St. Louis marked the boundaries of the imaginable world. South was the Lake of the Ozarks, fantailed through the low mountain chain, where young people went mostly in groups. Real cosmopolites went as far south as Lake Taneycomo, near the Arkansas border. North? Well, we could and did go to Marshall or Moberly or Mexico, but those were merely places on a map, not in the imagination. North just didn't exist. St. Joseph, north and west of Kansas City, had the third largest population in Missouri, but I can't remember anyone from my town going there. Same with Cape Girardeau southeast, Joplin southwest.

Perhaps it required more imaginative effort to get to the edges of the world because the intervening space was more densely occupied. For one thing, the roads, however good, were all two-lane, and except for the flat stretch in the bottoms across the river, they curved and rose and climbed, so that driving required constant alertness and passing a good deal of adrenaline. Landmarks became more important because they helped to measure not only progress in space but, relative to the next reasonably flat stretch, the projected rate of speed. The senses were more engaged—particularly the sense of smell on the long hill just west of the Lamine River past the rendering plant, where the truck that collected dead animals brought them to be converted into by-products that I didn't want to know about.

And because, with very rare exceptions, the highways ran right through the middle of every town, it took longer to get through them as well as to them. As a result, you paid more attention to details, and because this was pre-franchise middle America, the stores and layout differed markedly from town to town. You got a sense of whole other ways of life lived by people superficially like you but oriented to different landmarks and institutions. You could imagine that life would be different in all sorts of incalculable ways if you lived there.

Even towns close enough to be familiar seemed a little exotic. New Franklin, three miles across the bottom land on the opposite bluff of the Missouri, was different from Boonville because the town had a real center—angle parking in the middle of the broad single block of its downtown—with a circle to drive around, a fire engine painted white rather than red, and a baseball field behind the school where they didn't always cut the grass in the outfield. Unlike Boonville, it was full of Democrats and had so few Catholics that the tiny church had no resident priest. The girls were reputed to be very daring. Prairie Home, to the southeast of Boonville in the German Lutheran half of Cooper County, had no Catholics at all, and the outfield in the baseball field behind their school wasn't quite level. But the town did have an annual fair, a drug store like a living museum, a lot of white frame houses, as opposed to Boonville's brick, and a high school gymnasium with a ceiling only five feet above the rim of the basket. Nobody I knew had ever gone out with a Prairie Home girl. Pilot Grove, southwest in the German Catholic half of the county, had a lot more beer joints and a bigger high school gym where its teams played ferociously well. They played softball rather than baseball. The girls were reputed to be very daring indeed.

You could go into these towns for a slightly different kind of meal—the cafe in New Franklin had particularly good homemade rolls—or just for a change of scene. Even towns off the state highway system like Bunceton supported a restaurant or two, a tavern, a high school, a bank—the infrastructure of a real town.

If you wanted to look up at taller buildings and people in them, you didn't have to go to the edges of the state. Columbia, just over twenty miles east, and Sedalia, a bit farther to the west-southwest, could serve for all but the most serious shopping expeditions. They had Sears stores and a wider range of shops than Boonville. And they offered other attractions. Columbia was the site of the University of Missouri and the glamor of big-time football, a journalism school, larger clubs more tolerant of underage beer-drinkers, and purportedly the very loosest kind of women, professional as well as amateur. Sedalia had the Missouri State Fair with harness racing, thousands of exhibits, and lightly clad dancing girls on the midway. Neither town reached a population of thirty thousand.

There was also a kind of human density that made movement difficult or unnecessary. Cooper County, mostly farm country, was (and is) not heavily populated, but descendants of long-term residents had a finely woven net of kinship, now a little wider in mesh, to hold and support them. My sister-in-law had fifty-one first cousins living in a ten-mile radius of Pilot Grove, and a family reunion revealed ties of kinship that newcomers like my family never suspected.

With all these relatives, family was a full-time occupation, especially for faithful churchgoers. There was a constant round of christenings, first communions, confirmations, weddings, and funerals. Weddings were major social events, the ceremony followed by a dinner for a lot of people and a dance for even more. Thanksgiving and Christmas dinners were extended family rituals. Less formal gatherings and visits were recorded in the social notes of the Boonville *Daily News.*

Then there was the part of church not formally connected with family—ordinary services, official feasts, and quasi-liturgical events like the crowning of the May queen. And purely social events, most of them connected with fund-raising, like picnics and socials and dances. The rule seemed to be, the smaller the parish, the bigger the event, so that the picnic at Martinsville, which had a Catholic church and grade school but no town at all, was one of the biggest in the county.

There were all kinds of auxiliary organizations, religious and secular, to take people out of the house to meet people they could see every day. My mother belonged to the Daughters of Isabella (honored, I suppose, because she staked Columbus), the women's side of the Knights of Columbus. Contrary to Protestant paranoid legend, the Knights didn't stockpile guns in the basement to prepare for a coup led by the Pope— they didn't have a basement. Besides sponsoring a Boy Scout troop and later a softball team in the city league, I don't know what the Knights did. I have no idea what the Daughters did.

My father had belonged to De Molay as a young man in Arkansas City, primarily because he could use them as cover to sponsor dances, but he had no interest in the Masons. He did belong to the Eagles, probably because they had a long-running poker game. When Grandpa

Murray moved to Boonville, he joined the Oddfellows, which seemed to me superfluous. Probably it gave him another audience. The service organizations, like the others, had national affiliations, but no one I knew held national office or even went to regional conventions.

In *A Portrait of the Artist as a Young Man*, young Stephen Dedalus moves from himself outward to the universe and realizes that "It was very big to think about everything." Even then, he was imagining a way out. But in my town, and probably in Dublin some fifty years earlier, social energy was centripetal, and the individual was defined by a series of labels that were impossible to unstick.

Everybody had a place in this world. If you weren't white, you were black. If you were black—not the term used, of course—you either "knew your place" or you didn't. In fact, almost everyone, white or black, knew not only his and her place but everybody else's. You were either Protestant or Catholic, Republican or Democrat, male or female, grown-up or child, respectable or trashy. You lived in town or on a farm. You either worked or you played. You drove an American-made car, and the make said a good deal not just about your income but about your conception of yourself and your role in society. Plymouth drivers were even more stolid than Chevrolet drivers. Ford drivers liked performance over reliability. Mercury drivers liked speed above all. Hudson drivers, at least after the war, preferred design to engineering. Those who bought Kaisers and Frasers were daring or desperate. The categories were invariable.

Everything had its place in time, too—at least in public, shared time. Despite the efforts of what weren't yet called futurists, time really meant the past. Not the official U.S. history we learned in fifth grade or the Missouri history we paid no attention to in high school. The authors of *1066 and All That* were wrong: history was not what you could re-member of the mass of dates, Good Things, and Bad Things. Nor was it what Studs Terkel thinks: personal oral history. At that time, history was what your family remembered.

And the family was denser, more compact, than most of us can imagine now. Unlike mine, most of them hadn't moved half a dozen times, so there were not only more tales but more artifacts—the kind that turn up with increasing and depressing regularity in local museums and antique shops, like cardboard milk bottle caps. Furthermore—and I don't think memory distorts that much—it seems to me that elders talked to us more than I did to my children, and not just in my incorrigibly anecdotal family. I certainly think that I listened more closely than my children seem to have. Anyway, it was a different kind of talk—anecdotes, testimonies, tales; the genre doesn't matter—woven into a whole web of narrative that differed for every family but essentially told the same version of twentieth-century American history.

The story ran backwards. And though now it may be hard to believe, the story did not begin with the Second World War because our fathers were too old and we and our siblings too young to have been anything but spectators. The real family story began with the Great Depression, all episodes concluding with "I hope you never have to go through anything like that." Like the generation just too young to have fought in the First World War, we weren't sure that we could be that strong and were just as glad that we would never be tested.

For me, the Depression meant that my Grandpa Murray had to go live on a farm in Morgan County in the Ozark foothills because he had lost his money and property in the stock market crash. If this could happen to the smartest man I knew, then some cataclysmic and unavoidable force had to be responsible. More comprehensible was the story of his and my father's trip to buy a truckload of pecans in Pauls Valley, Oklahoma, to bring back and sell in Arkansas City, Kansas— and having to eat them all. This story gave a real point to my mother's often-repeated dietary law: "Beans (or X) is what we got; beans is what we'll eat." But the story defied common sense, because I had never seen and could not imagine those two men unable to sell anything they chose.

The twenties, before our parents married and we came along, sounded like a lot more fun than the forties, during which the twenties had a nostalgic vogue. I knew why Prohibition failed: Mom's settled belief that the heavy, sweet taste of Dr. Pepper was good only for disguising moonshine's sublethal qualities. I knew why gangs flourished: gangsters started out selling booze in places like Arkansas City—in fact, my father's first real job was pressing pants and serving as a lookout for the cleaner/bootlegger's temperance union wife. One of their high school classmates was found floating face down in Boston harbor, but that was a cost of doing that kind of business, not a social or even a personal tragedy. A road block for Pretty Boy Floyd in southeastern Kansas almost nailed my parents, who were bringing home from Missouri a trunkload of booze in a car the same make and color, though a different model, than the one Floyd was reported to be driving. Grandpa told stories about helping to move bootleg booze into the Cowley County courthouse and seeing fellow officials stash confiscated bottles in the hedge surrounding the lawn. I got the impression that he did not reject this highly unofficial finder's fee. What about the non-drinkers? We probably knew some, but they didn't make good stories.

Before the twenties started to roar was a period when anything might happen, a world that could be partly defined by subtracting from the sum of the present—cars, sound movies, electric lights, indoor plumbing. But there were also bank robbers like the ones Grandpa had chased and confrontations like his with the gas company.

The pretwenties was the period of our parents' childhood, full of stories like the one beginning, "By God, when I was your age, I used to get up at 4 o'clock and meet that Santa Fe train and carry the Wichita *Eagle*." God being merciful in those days, He provided older sisters, aunts who could correct or augment accounts like these. It seems that Dad had left out the pony who pulled the cart and knew the route so well that he would stop until Dad woke up and threw a paper at each stop. Not every father's "when I was a boy" story started this profanely, but everybody's father seemed to have one. I have some myself, though they seem rather pale, and when my children complained about some hardship, like black-and-white television, imposed on them, I pointed out that this would give them something to lie to their grandchildren about. But when I was a boy, the stories of youthful ordeals were as vivid to me as genre paintings. Mostly, though, the verbal and literal pictures in boxes and albums showed people doing things we could understand in an almost pastoral, Booth Tarkington way that we could deal with.

The Second World War was not history because we could remember it—or at least the newsreel, newspaper, and Hollywood accounts of it. Candy had been hard to get, we remembered, and some of us had to stand in line to get cigarettes for our parents—not Twenty Grand, my mother would implore or lament. Ration books for meat, shoes, gas, and maybe sugar had been a fact of life. You took stamps out of those and put stamps in savings bond booklets. You helped gather milkweed pods so that the floss could be used in life jackets. You collected aluminum foil in larger and larger balls to give to the war effort. Some of the other kids may have had relatives in the war, but I didn't know any. And when the atomic bombs dropped on Hiroshima and Nagasaki, most of us just felt relieved.

Anyway, with the war over, the past had ended happily. Nobody we knew well had died. We had always had the same pope, as far as I knew, and for a long time the same president, and we had the feeling that Franklin Delano Roosevelt had not so much died as been apotheosized. Everyone had lived through the flu epidemic because my grandfather had turned on the gas for Arkansas City, and he never went to jail or shot anybody and, more important to us, nobody had ever shot him. He never recovered all of his property, but he never lost his enthusiasm. My father's scar from the failed romance and my mother's various broken arms from riding accidents had healed, and though my father had been abandoned in both desert and mountains, he had probably got what he deserved, or so I liked to believe, and anyway he had managed to find his way home. Nobody my generation knew had died from gang or police bullets or got jake-leg from rotgut whiskey. Though the Depression had marked the older generation and, through example more than precept, us in ways that even now it is hard to calculate or overestimate, it had ended because of Roosevelt or the war, depending on whether you listened to my father, the lone Democrat in the Boonville branch of the family, or all the Republicans on my mother's side. We could see for ourselves that the good guys had won the war, just as the Hollywood westerns and war movies had assured us they would.

The future? Everyone seemed to feel that the present was a very good place to be, considering all the excitement we had had up until now.

Grown-ups and Kids

Some day I am going to have to tell you what life is all about," my father said to me. We were about a third of the way up Golf Course Hill. I could come within twenty yards of picking the spot forty-five years later.

I wasn't sure that I was ready to deal with anything that comprehensive, but I realized that sooner or later I was going to need that kind of information. I was surprised that it could be conveyed—not as briefly as the "Shazam" that turned Billy Batson, orphan newsboy, into Captain Marvel, superhero and copyright infringer of Superman. But my father was not a voluble man, so it might not be much longer.

Since I can't have been more than ten, it never occurred to me that he was probably talking about sex. He never mentioned the subject again.

Nor did it occur to me that he might not have the answer. Grown-ups obviously knew that sort of thing. Probably they wouldn't tell me, and when they indicated that they were passing on inside information, I couldn't understand or believe it. Actually, like most kids I made an unconscious distinction between grown-ups and parents. Parents were part of the family story, so that there was evidence, or at least testimony from people, who might exaggerate but had never, as far as I could tell, flat out lied to me, that they had once been children. Besides, the stories about Dad delivering papers and finding his way back from the desert and running off to work in the oil fields and about Mom's riding difficult horses and making her date walk home fit my understanding of their resoluteness and independence and pure-dee hogheadedness as grown-ups. It was even possible that the aunts and uncles had been children.

It was even assumed, though not often by me, that someday I would be a grown-up. By this time, though I didn't look any more like my father, grown-ups had found a precedent for my physical traits and even my eccentricities in Grandpa Murray, who was nearsighted, bookish, argumentative, and insatiably curious. But these traits didn't look characteristic of most adults I knew. And there were some other problems. For one thing, since as far as I could tell Grandpa had always been exactly the way he was, there was no way that I could become really like him. For another, he seemed to enjoy things that I could understand. For another, he didn't seem to care whether I was like him or not, and he talked to me the way he talked to everyone else, so that he was either treating me as a grown-up or treating grown-ups as kids.

I did realize that to be a real grown-up, I would have to function in the world outside the family. That seemed even more unpleasant than unlikely. In fact, impossible. There didn't seem any way to get to be a grown-up because no grown-up had ever been a kid. One might occasionally say that he had been, and it was impolite as well as pointless to argue with him, but I knew that it couldn't be true because if he had ever been a kid, he wouldn't be doing what he was doing now.

For one thing, grown-up men seemed to be linked with grown-up women, and it was hard for me to see the point of women. (Girls, a separate issue, I'll deal with later.) At that place and time, some feminists might grudgingly agree. For one thing, it was hard to figure out what women did. Food appeared; clothes got washed; husbands and kids got sent off to wherever they went for the day; bridge got played.

But the mothers of my friends seemed stuck inside their individual houses, June Cleavers waiting in the womb of time. It would have been presumptuous for me, as a kid, to feel sorry for them, so I just tried not to think about them.

Perhaps they only seemed boring and limited in contrast to my mother, who got out of the house as fast and as often as she could. She smoked constantly, would take a drink if it was offered, loved to dance, read all kinds of books (I don't remember seeing reading matter in friends' houses, except for *Popular Mechanics* at Jerry Lammers's), and would do things impulsively just for fun. Clearly not a grown-up. Like Grandpa Murray, she had a sharp-edged sense of humor and an independence of mind that sometimes made her uncomfortable in supporting social and religious pieties. I could argue with her and sometimes even win. She could whistle.

In fact, none of us kids had much contact with grown-up women outside the home. (Nuns were different—more later.) Before I went to school, my mother would take me up the steep, single flight of stairs to Powell Clayton's beauty shop above my father's pool hall. The shop seemed cramped and too brightly lit, and there was nothing for a kid to do. Even the pictures in the magazines had no interest for me. The sharp, acrid smell seemed to fit with the conversation, which sounded like nothing I had ever heard or ever heard again until I started going to academic parties. I can't remember what the women said. The dialogue in the stage play and film *Steel Magnolias*, set in a smalltown southern beauty shop, was far too pleasant and supportive to resemble their conversation, which was closer in spirit to *The Bacchae*. I can't remember any of the words, but the tone remains, and I could still hum a few bars. Some of it was funny, most of it was vicious, and all of it seemed designed to support a view of respectability in clothes and actions that seemed petty when it wasn't thoroughly confusing. The stories exhibited a kind of energy, but none of the enthusiasm of those my family told. Grown-up life, it seemed, was nasty and brutish and claustrophobic, and women fared no better than men in this beauty parlor version of life. Even then I wondered how Powell Clayton, the only other male in the room, stood it all day, every day.

The pool hall downstairs smelled a little odd, what with the beer and calf brains frying for sandwiches, but the long stretch of the room and the high ceilings provided plenty of space, comfortably dim except for the pools of light over the tables. The men seemed like a different species from the beauty parlor patrons. Chalky White, the fry cook at the lunch counter in the front corner, is the only one I remember as an individual. He had been a derelict ex-riverman until Dad gave him a job and bought him some teeth. We were new to town, but we already had an old family retainer. The other men blur together in my memory into a lean composite figure wearing a hat indoors with a cigarette hanging from one corner of the mouth. That figure didn't tell me how cute I was, and except for when he was teaching me to shoot pool or giving me something to eat or drink, didn't pay much attention to me.

Nobody was respectable, at least while he was in the pool hall. This was restful. The basement was intermittently respectable. Dad ran a poker game down there which, at a signal from Chalky, would turn into an innocent rummy game before the police could get down the stairs. The police must have come fairly often—not because gambling was illegal but because Dad was a newcomer—since later, when Dad played rummy with me, he always won handily.

Other places where grown-up men gathered smelled a little different—Lucky Tiger hair oil at the barbershop; grease and metal in the workspace of a garage, dust and dry paper in the cramped office; musty feed and eggs at my uncle's store in Otterville. Cigarette smoke was pervasive. In all of these refuges, the conversation might seem mysterious or pointless, but at least it was not scary. The tone was deeper and the tempo slower than the talk at the beauty shop, with lots of pauses. I liked it best when no one paid any attention to me. Sometimes, especially a little later, I was embarrassed by the assumption that I was on the verge of sharing grown-up urges, but I would pretend to be ignorant and more often was ignorant.

The problem with grown-ups, even men, was that there didn't seem to be any point to them. When they were working, they seemed incomprehensible. When they were having fun, they were messy and embarrassing. Fortunately, past a certain age—about first grade in my case—kids didn't have to spend a lot of time with grown-ups. Boonville was small enough that a kid not only could but was expected to walk anywhere he needed to go—school, movie, friend's house, playground, library—and he couldn't get into any real trouble as long as he remembered to watch out for the traffic. My mother may have had a higher or earlier tolerance for wanderlust than most, but then I had a good sense of direction and a built-in time clock, and though my brother often failed to turn up, it was because everyone knew and accepted the fact that his sense of direction was better than his sense of purpose. But by the time we were ten or twelve, all of us had a great deal of freedom.

At least we thought so. In fact, we were a minority—and given the demographics of 1933 and 1934, with the lowest birth rate in U.S. history until the late seventies, not an especially significant minority. The term "teenager," as currently used, did not come into the language in time to do us any good. There may have been a generation gulf, and we were on the wrong side, but there was no generation gap because we had no sense of being a generation. We were just kids. Meanwhile, the best way to get along was to avoid grown-ups when you could and say "Yessir" and "No ma'am" when you couldn't.

It didn't seem hard to avoid them, partly, I now realize, because grown-ups wanted us out of the way. There were lots of places to do that—basements; banks of the creeks that ran behind back yards in a no man's land. As we got older or bolder, the environs of Harley Park and, beyond it, the Old Brewery, a roofless ruin reportedly full of copper-heads and poison ivy; railroad tracks; barnyards and fields of nearby farms where classmates lived; the tops of the pilings of the bridge to which we could climb, when we got brave enough, from the pedestrian crosswalk. There wasn't anything to do once we got down there, but we had an agreeable sense that no one knew where we were. There was an island, now merged with the shore, at the far end of the bridge, which we reached by climbing over driftwood caught on the pilings. By this time I had read *Tom Sawyer*, and I thought of it as Jackson's Island, a place where we could be entirely free from adult supervision. We were less enterprising than Tom and his friends, but we could cut down the tall, slender trees and try to make wigwams. This turned out to be so much work that I don't think we ever finished one.

Until I began to remember in detail, it seemed to me that the distinction between grown-ups and kids was the only one recognizable. But grown-ups soon began to fall into classes and groups. There were, in my mother's formulation, "Negroes, niggers, white trash, and plain trash," in descending order. There were men and "old men." This term could be a description or a title of great respect, given only to the wise, clever, and highly individual. In Boonville, I knew three of them: Old Man Darby, who was my father's senior trading partner in buying farms; Old Man Melton, editor and publisher of the *Cooper County Record*, a licensed gadfly; and Old Man Murray, my grandfather. Monsignor Roels, our parish priest, would have been an Old Man except for the fact that priests were not really men. Old Men outranked grown-ups and assistant priests and had equal precedence with pastors.

The title could be used in public (defined as adults being present) only by grown-ups. The term "old lady" did not carry the same connotation. It was applied cautiously, even by grown-ups, to women like the elderly sisters catty-corner from our house on Sixth Street who wore sunbonnets and confiscated balls that fell into their yard.

There was also—still is, in different terms—a recognized hierarchy among kids—"pecking order" gives the wrong impression, because the lower orders had enough sense to stay out of the way and the taller orders thought it beneath their dignity to notice the lower even to persecute them. The caste lines seemed rigid at the time, but in fact you moved up in stages unmarked by rites of passage, realizing the movement only after the fact.

At the bottom of the order were "little kids." They didn't have clothes; their mothers dressed them up, accounting for the most embarrassing photos in family albums. They wore a lot of hats. Knickers. Galoshes with lots of buckles. If they had wheels at all, they rode tricycles or miniature automobiles with pedals that always got locked or took you backward when you wanted to go forward. Tricycles and scooters worked better, but they were toys rather than modes of transportation. You never saw them alone or even in a group. If the family had a dog, the dog went with the little kid to watch over him. (My first dog, a Spitz, had a long white tail that signaled my location to Mom.) Little kids didn't really know how to have fun, so they tried to hang around bigger kids, who did. You often saw them with one or both parents. They had high voices and tended to fall down a lot. Officially, boys stopped being little kids when they got old enough to be Cub Scouts, for me about 1943, but in fact it all depended on physical dexterity and mental independence.

Then there was the category of "just kids." The point about being a Cub Scout was that you were assumed to be capable of handling a real knife, taking group trips, and if you fell or, more frequently, were knocked down, were capable of getting up and either being stoically silent, retaliating, or requesting minor forms of first aid. Just kids had graduated from tricycles to real bicycles, and this was an even bigger challenge than a knife because bicycles meant pretty much 26-inch wheels with balloon tires—and a boy's bike, since every self-respecting male preferred the inconvenience and occasional pain of the cross-bar to the ignominious comfort of a girl's bike. (My father had somehow discovered a 20-inch Schwinn bike, which he bought me for my sixth or seventh birthday, and for years grown-ups in Cooper County mar-veled at what was obviously a real bike but was kid-sized, and all the kids wanted to ride it.) You didn't have to have a bike to get around Boonville—my town friends lived only a few blocks from school, down-town, and everywhere else, and I lived at most a mile and a half away, despite what I tell my children—but it certainly increased your range, for once you had a bike, you were tacitly permitted to go anywhere you had the nerve to go and the strength to get back from by yourself. You didn't have to go, but you knew that you could. You learned some dirty words, though not necessarily what they meant. Mothers still bought clothes for kids in this category, but they didn't, except for state occa-sions, dress them (and even then, compare photos of first communions with those of confirmations, which look far less like uniforms and more like dress clothes). Mothers of this category tended to say, plaintively, "How come you never wear that cute yellow shirt (or whatever tasteless garment that had been relegated to the bottom and back of the lowest drawer) I got you?"

You didn't change from just a kid to a "big kid" overnight. First you stopped playing hide-and-go-seek and cowboys and Indians with the neighborhood children, including younger brothers. You moved, if starting from or inclined in that direction, from Cub to Boy Scouts (1946 in my case), from hikes to overnight (and in my view very uncomfortable) camping trips. The local movie theaters started charging adult prices at twelve, and you stopped going to the Saturday matinees because cowboy movies seemed a little dumb and anyway, since you were gradually allowed out of the house at night, it seemed a pity not to go to a movie because there was almost nothing else to do. You didn't stop going to church, but you stopped going with your parents (Catholics, anyway, had some choice because there were more services). You began to choose your own clothes and even developed a parodic sense. I still remember fondly a gold satin bowling shirt I acquired in an attempt to cure my mother of her fondness for yellow. It failed because she had a sense of humor, rare for a grown-up and almost unknown among grown-up women. You developed an interest in organized sports, learning to root for the St. Louis Cardinals and the Missouri Tigers if you had any regard for decent opinion. Girls started to smell better. It seemed achingly possible that someday you might learn to drive a car and even own one. You were almost never seen with an adult and spent more and more time hanging out with "the gang," a much more innocent term than now. Dirty words began to acquire content. You even began to develop some individual tastes. Some of us who were more dextrous or who had fathers who were handy learned to build things out of wood and even metal. Some of us (me) read. You spent a lot less time being bandaged or sewn up or having medicine and thermometers thrust at you.

In fact, it seems to me that I can trace the stages of my development by various scars. The one on the side of my left thumb—in fact, it helped me learn left from right—came from falling out of a wagon being pulled too fast by some bigger kids. The one by my right armpit I got from jumping off a merry-go-round to meet my mother, who was picking me up from kindergarten. The one on my left heel came from getting it caught in the back wheel of a baby-sitter's bicycle and was the reason I started the first grade on crutches. Those were little kids' kinds of wounds.

The one on the knuckle of my left thumb came from whittling toward myself with a knife, and the very faint one on my right ring finger was the result of my attempt to catch a barn cat I had cornered under a stall, a question of who caught whom. That was a little kid's trick, but I cleaned and bandaged the wound myself because I was too embarrassed to admit what had happened. The scar on my left hand where a schoolmate deliberately scratched me seems to have faded. Those were kids' injuries.

In the next stage I picked up the one by my right elbow playing basketball at a scout meeting, pulling my arm across a friend's tenderfoot pin as I grabbed a rebound. Since I can't see under my beard, I don't know if I pared off in all those years of shaving the one on my chin from a line drive off Leroy Vollmer's bat during a Sunday afternoon pickup game. The one on my left knee I got throwing a rolling block at Bill Harlan while practicing base-running in a game of run-up. Damned if I know where I got the one on the top of my left thumb.

And this isn't counting various bike wrecks, falls, collisions, playground fights, encounters with righteous nuns, and experience of my father's wrath. No wonder American men become stoics. They have a lot of practice.

Anyway, about the time we got off the recurring injury list, it began to penetrate to the edges of our consciousness that we were going, like it or not, to be grownups some day. It didn't occur to us, I think, that there was any pattern except those set for us by our fathers. One friend, attempting to nudge us forward, started calling each of us by his respective father's first name—fairly daring, since the first names of adults might appear on signs and mailboxes but were not to be spoken aloud by kids except to identify themselves by family to strange grown-ups.

(I knew my father not only by his official names, first "M.C." and then, at some point, "Matt," but also by his childhood nickname—but when he died, I was in my fifties, and even in thinking about him I don't use anything but Dad.)

We began to ape adult habits. When we were just kids, we went down to the creeks to build dams and try to catch tadpoles. Now we hid out in the culverts to cough in smoke from rolled or store-bought cigarettes— Camels were a real man's smoke—and an occasional cigar. (We didn't even hear about marijuana until we were old enough to be jazz fans.) Somebody got hold of a bottle of Virginia Dare bar sour which we carried over to the island and tried to sip. It tasted as bad as the whiskey my uncle and his friends had let me taste at the Otterville grain eleva- tor when I was a little kid, and a lot worse than beer, but its effects were so disappointing that I don't think we even pretended to be drunk.

Some of us even got the kind of jobs available at that time—working at soda fountains, stocking shelves at drug and grocery stores, throwing the Boonville *Daily News*, cutting grass, doing chores if you lived on a farm or, like me, on the edge of town—but that didn't teach us much about what grown-ups did at work. We began to feel grown-up when we got our drivers' licenses. No test. All you had to do was be sixteen, which I hit in 1950, no time off for good behavior, though most country kids had been driving for some time. A 1991 TV commercial blares, "It's not just your car; it's your freedom." We knew all about that. When we learned to drive, we began to appear in public more often, driving up Main Street and making a U-turn in the driveway of Cleary's Standard Service Station next to the bridge and back down again. Some big kids (we substituted "guys" for that term) even bought vehicles older than we were that looked like parodies of grown-up cars: the 1933 Chevy with doors opening from the front rather than the back; the 1925 Baby Overland coupe with a box-bed inserted where the rumble-seat used to be; most exotic of all, the 1931 Gardner that looked like something out of a gangster movie, had a cigar lighter attached to an elastic band (which, when released from the back seat, made a satisfying thump), and used more oil than it did gas. Jerry Koester was told at the license bureau that if he bought one more car, he would have to get a dealer's license. It was amazing how many guys could get into one of these vehicles and how naturally your place in the car—front seat, back seat, top layer, bottom layer—reflected your status in the group and with the driver.

By the time I was one of the guys, Dad was trading used cars out of our big back yard. Today some of his stock would be called classic, but then they were just old. They had an amazing variety of equipment. Once I ran down the battery of an old Buick because I couldn't figure out how to turn off the running lights attached to the front window posts. (Turn the ring surrounding the horn button.) After I had a series of minor breakdowns, Dad lamented that every time I went out something went wrong. I responded that if he ever let me drive something that didn't have wooden spokes on the wheels, I might have better luck. Later, when I was driving on a triple date to Columbia, he told me to be home by 10 P.M. and not to drive over forty miles an hour. Bold or foolhardy, I answered, "Dad, I can do one or the other, but I can't do both." Even he could see the sense in that, and it was the first time I ever talked him out of anything. I felt almost grown-up.

Grown-up enough to start going with my friends to bars across the river and trying, five years under age, to buy beer and to act sophisticated.

But in fact, though the gulf got wider between us and the little kids and narrower between us and the grown-ups, it still existed. There began to seem some point in being a grown-up because they had all the power.

For the most part, grown-ups exercised a benevolent tyranny. If you were white and middle-class and not too outrageous (raiding gardens or fruit trees was inside the line; flat-out stealing was beyond it), the cops would call your parents to get you back in line. Neighbors and family friends turned out to have you under observation at the most surprising and inconvenient times—which was why even the youngest just kids were allowed to wander around Boonville. But the really annoying thing about adults was that they were almost always there, and when they were there, they were always right.

Any adult who wasn't black or obvious white trash had the right, in fact the obligation, to yell at any kid for any reason. The reverse was almost unthinkable. Once, when I was riding my Monkey Ward 26-inch bike at top speed down Locust Street Hill to build up momentum for the opposite slope, Mrs. Klenklen (I think her name was Laureen, but the taboo on first names for grown-ups worked) pulled away from the stop sign at Seventh Street without noticing oncoming traffic. I had to skid my bike sideways to avoid broadsiding her. In surprise and with a surge of adrenaline—I was by this time a biggish kid—I yelled something like, "Watch where you're going." By the time I had covered the mile between me and home, she had called my mother to report that I had been disrespectful and apparently expected an apology. I pointed out to Mom with some heat that Mrs. Klenklen's carelessness might have killed me, and since Mom was only a part-time adult, the matter was allowed to drop. The fact that Mrs. Klenklen had done something stupid was apparently never pointed out to her.

To be fair, though, most of the times we got yelled at, "called down," or spoken to more in sorrow than in anger, we deserved it for being destructive, noisy, or obnoxious. One of our problems was that we didn't know how to join the adult world we knew. We had to imagine other roles from very slender materials and try to play them without scripts. Or maybe this was just my problem. Anyway, that is another part of the story.

Blacks and Whites

When my family moved to Boonville, I was four years old, and I don't know that I had ever seen a black person. Arkansas City, Kansas, where we had lived most recently and where my parents grew up, obviously had some because their pictures taken for the yearbook of the integrated school appeared at the back of the book. Boonville certainly had some—in fact, Cooper and Howard counties, facing each other across the river, had had slave populations among the highest in Missouri; not all the blacks had moved away, and the area was still called Little Dixie.

In fact, a few black families lived in the alley behind us, and one of them had a little boy who was called by initials that didn't stand for anything. Aside from this virtue, he knew about the private dump of Kemper Military School where the boys, incredibly old and rich by our standards, discarded treasures like books of maps interleaved with tracing paper and a lot of other neat stuff. Since I was new in the neighborhood, I was glad to have someone to hang out with.

I can't say that he was a playmate, since I don't remember us playing, and he clearly wasn't a friend because it was unthinkable—in the sense that it never occurred to either of us—that one of us would go inside the other's house. I don't know if my mother knew that I associated with him, for I never saw him on Third Street. His mother might have known, since I would walk to his house in the alley.

I don't remember when or why we stopped our association, but it may have been when I met some of the white kids in the neighborhood. The first I didn't meet so much as encounter—a poor white named Cecil (I thought of him for years as "Seasel," which seemed a lot more sinister), who took away the money I was carrying to buy candy at Hopkins's store a block away.

The other white kids weren't much more restful. Early on, the kids who lived on Third Street had a brief war with the kids who lived up the hill in fancier houses. This war involved BB guns, shorter range missiles, and some noise. Assuming that no one would be suspicious of a little kid, they co-opted me to infiltrate the plutocrats and report on their arsenal. I did get into their clubhouse—a shed in someone's back yard—and reported that they had a box of rocks. But I decided that big white kids were trouble, a view that changed only ten years later when I put on a growth spurt and became a big white kid myself.

At some point in that summer the grown-ups decided to send me to Arkansas City and New Mexico. Probably, as I've said, this was to give some relief to my mother, pregnant with my brother, but I saw it as a real adventure. The logistics were a little complicated: Mom and Dad drove me to Sedalia, where I took an overnight train to Wichita, to be met by my aunt Nanelou for a bus trip to Arkansas City and another bus to Albuquerque. My parents gave me some money, which I welcomed, and lots of advice, which I immediately forgot. What I do remember is feeling enormously important at taking a train trip all by myself and secretly relieved at the attention given me by a large black woman. I realized years later that Mom and Dad must have paid her to look after me, but she did it so well that I never realized it. Because of her, the grown-ups regarded me as exceptionally self-reliant and not only allowed but encouraged my independence.

After that, I didn't associate with blacks for a long time. We moved from Third Street, but never near any of the other pockets reserved for blacks, and I became gradually aware that blacks were confined to these areas. This was confusing to my sense of social hierarchy because there weren't just grown-ups and kids but black and white divisions of each class. It has taken me fifty years even to begin to understand how confusing it has been not just for me but for all people of good will in both races.

This was an intellectual problem rather than a social one because most white people didn't have to deal with blacks very often. Boonville public schools were segregated until my younger companion from the alley reached high school age, was allowed to enroll at Laura Speed Elliott, and much improved the basketball team. One talented black girl was allowed to come to the convent of the teaching sisters for music lessons. But then nuns could get away with anything. No blacks attended the Catholic school, but then no one had ever heard of blacks being Catholics.

The town was segregated socially, though not, as far as I could tell, legally. That is, there weren't separate restrooms or drinking fountains for blacks in public places, but in fact this meant that blacks couldn't get a drink of water or use the restrooms. The only blacks in white restaurants were carrying food or cleaning it up, not eating it. Blacks were allowed to sit at the rear of the balcony in the Lyric Theater, but the Casino, smaller and with a single floor, had no place to put them. (When *The Jackie Robinson Story* came to town in 1950, the Casino got the booking and the manager held a special showing for blacks only.) I wasn't aware of any white violence toward blacks, and despite rumors about the black nightclub tucked under the bridge, not much black violence toward blacks.

The black person closest to my extended family was a very neat and competent man named Dan who worked for my uncle Bob, first in his feed store and then in his lumber yard in Otterville. I never knew his last name or if he was married. He was calm, quiet, and dignified—

qualities not conspicuous among my relatives—and the closest thing we ever had to an old family retainer. You could rely on him, but I never had the sense that you could get to know him.

As newcomers, my parents had a different attitude from long-term white natives of Boonville. My mother certainly had prejudices: "poor white trash" was a phrase she used frequently, and she would drop the first adjective if economic circumstances warranted it. This class ranked below blacks, in her view. But by the standards of her in-laws, she was a Yankee, born in Evansville, Indiana, and descended from a Union soldier who had been in a Confederate prison. She wasn't a flaming liberal, but her racial attitudes seemed a little unconventional.

My father was born and raised in Kansas, but he was definitely a southerner and used the vocabulary. Once, describing to an eastern liberal colleague a rare letter I had received from him, I could not re-member what he had called a black colleague on the city council: "It wasn't 'nigger,' but I can't remember what it was." Horrified, my col-league asked if my father would *say* "nigger." Oh, yes, he'd say it. But he wouldn't *write* it.

I'm not even sure that he *thought* it in any real sense. He was capable of equally intense loyalties and antipathies, but he didn't seem to gen-eralize about religion, class, or region, and I don't think that, allowing for his upbringing, he did about gender or race. (Maybe that general trait got handed down. My daughter once asked her mother what a male chauvinist was. Given a detailed answer, she observed, "Dad isn't one of those. Dad feels that way about everybody.") For years he had used a black plumber, Hadley Briscoe, and when Hadley died, Dad went to his funeral. This was a real concession, not because the funeral was in a black church but because it was in any kind of church. He seemed to value people like Hadley who did what they said they would do when they said they would do it, black or white.

The only difference I could see was that poor blacks were more interesting than poor whites. The most colorful man in Boonville was a large black called Weatherbird. I think his last name alliterated, but black last names were almost as taboo as grown-up white first names. I don't know what Weatherbird did for a living, but everyone in town knew him by sight—large and solid, wearing bib overalls—and especially by sound, for he could whistle a piercing, melodious trill like nothing I have heard since. And he always seemed cheerful and relaxed, a kind of black Falstaff. Even then, I found it hard to see why.

The blacks we talked to indoors were Red and Leroi (my spelling; his Missouri version of French pronunciation), waiters at Pete's Cafe. Red really did have reddish hair and a light cast to his skin, but he moved and talked black. Leroi was darker, but he didn't move or talk like any blacks we knew, or for that matter like any whites. He was sinuous, precise in speech, elegant, and, toward gaggles of white teen-agers, almost supercilious. We tried to make the pronunciation of his name into a joke, but he was so confident that we couldn't. Years later, when I read Jean-Paul Sartre on customers trying to reduce a waiter to his role, I thought of Leroi, who insisted so strongly on his position as a waiter that he transcended the social and racial limitations that Boonville tried to impose. There were rumors about the exact nature of their friendship, but to me, the oddest thing about Red and Leroi was the story that they had left Boonville—and then come back. That didn't make any sense to me at all.

Some of us who delivered newspapers knew the twins, Melvin and Marvin, who carried the Kansas City *Times* and *Star*. They were legendary because they had routed Pete Christus's dog, reportedly the meanest in town. One of them rode the bicycle while the other, sitting on the crossbar, clobbered the dog with a brick. But we got the story at third hand because, though we might say hello to them, we didn't *talk* to them.

These blacks seemed like static characters because we associated them with one setting and one kind of activity, and when they were offstage, so to speak, they did not exist, and they did not seem to have a future or a past. Lefty Smith was different. He had been in prison— burglary, I think—and I knew him because "Hap" Schlotzhauer, the local Buick dealer for whom my father was sales manager and my mother bookkeeper, had given him a job washing and detailing cars. Lefty was a good worker and a pleasant and cheerful man, but I paid particular attention to him because he was a very good player on the local black baseball team and I badly wanted to be a ballplayer myself. On and off the mound, Lefty moved with an ease and confidence that I didn't have a word for until I encountered *panache*. (There wasn't much call for the term in Boonville, and none at all in the white community. My grandfather came closest to having it, but he was a little too abrupt in speech and movement.)

But Lefty did have a past—and a future of sorts. The story I heard was that he was having some kind of trouble with a woman who either wanted more money coming in or him going out. So he took a cab to a spot near an isolated store, had the driver wait, and broke into and robbed the store. He was arrested, of course, and sent back to the prison at Jefferson City. I couldn't see how anyone could be that desperate, but clearly he had been, and a little corner was lifted on a whole different world. Unlike Huck Finn realizing that Jim could care as much for his children as a white man could, I didn't experience any sudden revelation. But I did begin to think better of blacks, and the reaction of whites to my reaction to blacks made me think a whole lot worse of them.

I came to be regarded as a liberal or, as many people phrased it, a "nigger lover" because of a case of measles that hit me during the 1941 World Series. Since I couldn't get out of bed and the room was kept dark to protect my eyes, I was left with the radio. I had never listened to a ball game before, and though I don't remember any of the details of the broadcasts, when I got out of bed I was a Brooklyn Dodgers fan for reasons I can't remember. Perhaps it was because, like my father's ancestors, they lost to the Yankees.

Deep in St. Louis Cardinal country, this was subversive and probably perverted behavior. But since the Cardinals beat the Dodgers in the first play-off in major league history in 1946, Cardinal fans could almost pity me. Then Branch Rickey, the Dodgers' general manager, brought Jackie Robinson to the major leagues. That had enormous effects on organized sports, beginning with the 1947 National League pennant for the Dodgers, and on the social fabric of the whole country. Locally, where I had heard a white woman criticized for letting her black cleaning lady ride in the front seat with her, it changed me from being a social aberration into a traitor to my race.

I'm not sure how much of this antipathy was directed at what they perceived as my racial attitudes and how much to their sense that I was different. Or how much of my racial attitude was the result of my sense that I was different. Years later, reading Mezz Mezzrow's *Really the Blues* and Norman Mailer's essay "The White Negro," I could see that these men had identified themselves with blacks in opposition to white society, Mezzrow to the extent that he listed his race as Negro. I was never prepared to go that far.

Between 1947 and the time I left for college in 1951, I was not exactly ostracized, and I was never assaulted, for that anyway, but for years some people used the nickname "Jackie" as a put-down until I got big enough to whip some and finally big enough to stare down the rest.

At first, I didn't like blacks any better, but I certainly hated my tormentors a lot more, and I figured that if all this white trash were against both of us, there might be something worth learning about Robinson. The most obvious thing, as the daily box scores in the Kansas City *Star* revealed, was that he was a very good and versatile baseball player. That first year, the Dodgers played him at first base, partly to protect him from opposition runners and partly to use Eddie Stanky, the short, white second baseman with more aggressiveness than natural talent who was traded to the Giants the next year or so.

But the box scores were less revealing than the newsreels which showed Robinson running bases in a way that no modern fan had ever seen. By 1947, base-stealing was almost a lost art. Today, when the records of Ty Cobb (a nasty white man if there ever was one) have been broken and rebroken by a series of very pleasant blacks, the "Who, me?" school of baserunning seems dominant; that is, the runner will edge carefully away from the bag, trying not to call attention to himself, and suddenly, at the last split second, break for the next base. Robinson (I wouldn't, for obvious reasons, use his first name) was different. He seemed to be saying, "You know I'm going to steal this base, and you can't stop me." He was especially impressive from third base, charging down the line on every pitch just far enough not to be picked off and, sometimes, often enough to set records, racing toward the plate to arrive safe in a cloud of dust. Unlike a lot of baseball players, he was a complete athlete, having starred in track and football, and when he arrived at home plate, he was encountering not a white man but an opposing catcher. How satisfying this must have been for him.

For me too. A few years later, I was playing baseball and even getting on base occasionally, and though I wasn't as big or fast as Robinson, but more like Eddie Stanky, I found his tactics very useful against teenage pitchers and catchers, especially from third base. I don't know that I ever stole home, but I scored a lot on wild pitches and passed balls. Like Tom Sawyer, I tried to throw a lot of style into it at a time when the chief object of the majority of people was to be as much like everyone else as possible.

That included the two black kids who played briefly with my team.

Zane—I don't remember his last name—moved so easily and surely at shortstop that he didn't need any extra style, and Henkle—I never learned his first name—was quiet and unobtrusive.

One area where blacks weren't at all like whites was music, which in the late 1940s must have reached its nadir. When else could a half-hour of radio time be devoted to the Hartz Mountain Canaries, thirty minutes of twittering to a pre-Muzak background? Or a song titled "Cincinnati Dancing Pig" become a hit? There was classical music, semiclassical music (that meant that the musicians wore tuxedos and you could recognize the tunes), popular music, which pretty much meant Guy Lombardo, and hillbilly music, which was beneath middle-class notice but not contempt. When the Catholic school started a band, I wanted to play the saxophone, but for some reason, probably because Dad got a better deal on a used trombone, I was stuck with that. Even if I had been able to play the saxophone, the band never played any music I thought worth listening to, let alone playing.

Then, too late to do anything for my musical career, I somehow dis-covered, probably in 1949 or 1950, the New Orleans Jazz Club program on WWL, a 50,000 watt clear-channel station (AM, of course) "high atop the Roosevelt Hotel." I had never heard anything like the drive and virtuosity of the jazz men, most of them black, and the announcer's commentary hinted that the music and musicians were part of a cul-tural and artistic process that I found exciting. While classical music had an even longer tradition, no one told me about it, and in any case I was finding it out for myself. This made the whole thing satisfying in a way that I had never experienced in school, church, or anywhere else.

About this time Dad took as part payment for a used truck a record player and a highly eclectic collection of 78 rpm records, including a version of "Going Down Slow" by Etta Jones backed by Luke Jones and His Five Joes, right on what I later realized was the fringe between straight blues and rhythm and blues. So there were a lot of things going on in the big world out there, which, as far as I could tell, no one in Boonville but me knew about or was interested in discovering. A little later, when I went to the local record store and asked for a Louis Armstrong record, it had to be special-ordered (*Louis Armstrong and His All-Stars*, including Barney Bigard, Jack Teagarden, Cozy Cole, and Arvell Shaw, on a 10-inch LP that I wore almost slick).

In case this doesn't mean much to a member of a younger generation, she or he should try to get hold of the 1940s version of "It's a Sin to Tell a Lie" by Something Smith and the Redheads, a white novelty group. Then listen to Fats Waller's version to discover what black music had that white didn't.

After I left Boonville, I knew some blacks—mostly Africans—in college, but not until graduate school did I talk to a young black woman and not until I got to Chicago in the early sixties did I see blacks—Muslims—better dressed and more confident than I, who clearly didn't care whether white people were around or not. This was confusing, because, while I applauded (silently) their attitude toward the white world, I wished that they would make an exception of me. A lot of other stuff has happened to make me cringe at memories of my condescending curiosity.

But the early conditioning dies hard. Unless I think about it, I assume that black strangers are going to be pleasant and nurturing and just plain nicer and more interesting than white strangers. When I see non-African blacks in Europe, I have to resist the assumption that they are fellow Americans.

Over the years, though, I learned something about the price blacks in Boonville had paid for seeming that nice. A newspaper I worked for in Great Bend, Kansas, would not, in 1955, print a photo I had taken of a black ballplayer because, the excuse ran, he wouldn't show up properly on newsprint. That same year, helping an African college classmate and his bride move across Kansas, I went into restaurants they couldn't enter and brought them food. And Kansas wasn't even what I had been taught to regard as the real South.

When I did see the real South, driving through Mississippi for the first time on the way to New Orleans in 1957, I got a sense of what it was like from the sharecropper cabins and segregated drinking fountains I had never seen, or perhaps never noticed before. On a train ride from Chicago to St. Louis in the early sixties, I listened to the black porter's accent become more obviously southern black with each stop, whether in mockery or protective coloration I could not tell because in those days I had one accent for graduate school in the north and another for working in Boonville.

A few years ago, visiting Greenville, Texas, not all that long after the city fathers had taken down the sign boasting of "the blackest land and the whitest people in America," I got some sense of what it must have been like to be black in Boonville. On the edge of town was a barbecue joint run by a family of blacks, the parents not much older than I, a son in the mid-teens. Listening to them talk, I felt as though I had entered a time warp. If they were playing humble, they were doing it so well that I couldn't catch them at it. They might not have thought that white people were superior, but they seemed to be acting as though they had to act like that was true. Thirty-five years after I thought I had left the system, I felt ashamed of what it was still doing.

Back in New Orleans in the mid-eighties, I felt a little better while talking to a black cabdriver. He hoped I had enjoyed my stay, and I replied that things certainly seemed different from my first trip in 1957.

"You can remember back that far?"

"Well, I was twenty-two—and I saw my first B-girl and my first segregated restrooms, and they blew my mind."

"I was sixteen then, and I had two kids and a wife. Lots of people don't remember—segregation, even slavery. They say, you mean you people was like the *pits*? Even old people don't remember."

"College students who are supposed to know history don't know."

"You telling *me*? A lot of changes since then. These young people say that things haven't changed. But they're wrong."

Just how much they had changed became clear during one of my visits to Boonville. My brother ran a general store—gas, groceries, liquor, sandwiches, bait, ammunition—about two miles from the edge of town, a handy place to hang out and see the people of various generations who remembered me. A lot of rough-and-ready, formulaic small-town crosstalk passed back and forth among men and a few women of all classes and conditions.

Except black—until one afternoon a well-built young black man came into the store with a controlled rush and called my brother a nigger. Instead of fainting or reaching for a weapon, my brother replied loudly and cheerfully and took the money for gas and a coke. Like most customers, the young man's visit seemed as much social as commercial, and after he swigged his coke he looked carefully at me, back at my brother, and back to me again and said, "You related to this character?" I admitted as much, and my brother, after confirming the fact, asked the young man how his baseball team was doing and added, to me, that he was a first-rate ballplayer.

"I used to play a little ball myself," I said. "In fact, I played on the first integrated team in Boonville with a black kid named Zane. He was the best shortstop we ever had."

"Oh, he's still playing, but he had to move to third base because he's slowed down a little. Still a pretty good ballplayer, though."

So we talked some baseball until that ran down, and then I remembered to ask about the little black kid I had played with in 1939.

"Him? Hell, he's not black—he's high yellow!"

"God damn it," I said, relieved not to have to be too polite to a black, "just about the time we learn some new words, y'all go and change them on us!"

"Well"—and this was the end of the only conversation I ever had with a black person in Boonville—"I'm glad you learned those words."

Protestants and Catholics

The story goes that a Catholic priest is walking along the street and encounters three boys sitting on the curb. The red-haired kid says, "Good morning, Father," followed immediately by the dark-haired kid and, after a pause, by the black kid. The priest asks each his name and if he is a Catholic. The first replies, "Jimmy Riley. Yes, Father, St. Bridget's parish." The second answers, "Frankie Torrelli. Yes, father, St. Lucy's Parish." The third: "Roosevelt Brown. No, father, I'm colored, and that's bad enough." The joke wasn't realistic—kids from different ethnic parishes probably wouldn't even know each other, and they probably wouldn't associate with a black kid—but it does show that Catholics thought of themselves as a minority, and by no means a privileged one.

In Boonville, there was no economic or social disadvantage to being a Catholic except that the church wouldn't let you join the Masons or the Order of the Eastern Star. The Germans who immigrated in the nineteenth century had obviously been hard-working and thrifty people, and their descendants had inherited everything but the language. Many of the prosperous farmers in the county had German names, and down Main Street, signs on the storefronts testified that Germans made successful burghers. Of course, most of them were not Catholics. But kids from the Catholic schools were supposedly in demand by employers of all faiths because we were honest, hard-working, and respectful of authority. (The older we got, the more clearly we saw that we did not get the higher-paying highway and construction jobs, but not until the mid-sixties, when I watched a Chinese-American revolt against the same stereotypes, did I realize what a disadvantage it was to be labeled as humble and biddable.) No single Protestant denomination had as many members, but except on Sunday, or so we assumed, they differed so little from each other that they were clearly the majority.

They didn't have to remind us of our minority status. The whole structure and doctrine of the Catholic Church convinced us that we were different not only on Sunday but every day of the week, and throughout eternity as well. In fact, Catholics of my generation may have been the last to have what Catholic intellectuals (a very period term) called a ghetto mentality. Our Sundays were spent differently; our eschatology was a lot more crowded; and our doctrines incredibly more complex than those of the Protestant majority around us. We even—like the blacks—went to segregated schools, though by choice.

In fact, we did not have a real choice because, as we were often reminded from the pulpit, it was a sin not to send your children to a Catholic school if one was available, and with very few exceptions one was always available. Because Catholic colleges were expensive even then, the hierarchy had begun to waffle about higher education, and of the four boys in my graduating class who went directly to college, two of us went to Catholic colleges (I was rescued at the last minute from the University of Missouri by a scholarship to Rockhurst, the nearest Jesuit college), one of us went to the university, and one began at Central Methodist, fourteen miles away in Fayette, before transferring to M.U. All the girls who continued their education went to Catholic nursing schools.

We were not supposed to attend Protestant services, and while exceptions were made for funerals or weddings, participation was frowned upon if not actually forbidden. This ban didn't seem much of a burden, since Protestants talked funny ("Gawd" seemed popular in their churches) and there was nothing much to look at, unlike our statues and candles of different sizes and colors and stained glass and different colored embroidered clothes—vestments—for the priest for different seasons and occasions, and nothing particular to smell unless you counted the flowers at funerals. And the hymns, while they had more singable tunes than most of ours, seemed even more simple-minded. Compared to Gregorian chant, even the way we sang it, the hymns seemed to lack aesthetic value, or, as we would have said, they didn't sound very impressive.

Catholics held on to their differences. We even had our own fears of spiritual miscegenation. It was a sin to marry a non-Catholic without special permission, given only after the unbelieving partner studied Catholicism and promised that all children would be raised as Catholics. (While it was not a sin to marry a black Catholic, the issue never arose in Boonville because there weren't any black Catholics in the first place and no one could imagine marrying a black person.) It wasn't exactly a sin to date non-Catholics, but it was definitely imprudent because dating could lead to marriage outside the Church or—Protestants were reputed to be oversexed and underinhibited—something worse. Actually, it wasn't worse. Although fornicating or even thinking in any detail about fornicating was a mortal sin, that could be taken care of fairly simply by confession. Marriage outside the Church meant automatic excommunication and a lot more hassle.

Even though a Good Catholic Marriage (we had more capital letters in those days) was officially sanctioned, the best possible way of life for a good Catholic boy or girl was to become a priest or nun. For most American Catholics, a religious vocation meant a rise not only in spiritual and social status—religious outranked even grown-ups—

but in intellectual and sometimes (in the case of priests in large and wealthy parishes) economic status.

All kinds of religious, a term applied to anyone who wore a uniform, or habit, and was called Father, Brother, or Sister, were supposed to be so much holier than the laity (as the rank and file were called) that they were scarcely human any more. A young priest remarked rather bitterly that many Catholics could not believe that priests went to the bathroom, and for a change I had sense enough to keep my mouth shut because I had just figured it out. The mystique of the religious, at least among Catholic grade-school children, was intended to create just this kind of attitude, useful because it disinclined us to ask awkward questions or any questions at all. Sort of like the Wizard of Oz—if we found out that they were just men and women, we might find it harder to believe that they had magic powers.

Moreover, the religious did in fact know things that the average lay person didn't because they had more if not always better education. And in those days education was a much rarer commodity than it is now. I knew that the parents of most of my classmates had never been to college, and those I'm not sure about never discussed the matter. Boonville had no Catholic lawyers, as far as I knew, and only two Catholic doctors, Dutch immigrant brothers, one of whom was so grand that he practiced in his own clinic rather than in the Catholic hospital staffed by a nursing order of nuns. So we had no intellectual class or even a real professional class, outside of the Van Ravenswaays, who were remote from our everyday experience, and Squinch Waldersheid, a druggist and fairly notorious alcoholic even by the town's exacting standards.

So that left the parish priest and his assistant to provide intellectual as well as spiritual leadership for the Catholics of the town. In fact, during most of my school years, we were lucky enough to have a pastor who was something of an intellectual, with a wider range of knowledge and a more complicated and subtler way of using it than anyone I knew in Boonville—except my atheist grandfather, who had a very different style. Any time a priest did or said something more than ordinarily stupid, Catholics were enjoined to respect the office rather than the man, but Father—later Monsignor—Roels seemed, to me at least, to confer dignity on his calling. His sermons stretched out to awesome proportions by Catholic standards. Unlike Protestants, Catholics scheduled more than one major service on Sunday, so priests had to move along to clear one church load and let in the next. Monsignor Roels left a lot of people in a holding pattern. People who went to the last mass and saw him come out of the sacristy groaned inwardly because they were going to be late for Sunday dinner, and, if they planned to go to Communion, they had been fasting since midnight. But so had he—and he seemed interested in what he was saying, thought it important if not always deadly serious, and put it in terms far removed from the simple-minded piety we sometimes heard.

But no matter what priest was on the altar performing the sacred rite that changed bread and wine into the body and blood of Christ, the barrier of the altar rail stood between him and the congregation. Not even nuns could enter the sanctuary while mass was being celebrated, though they and the ladies of the Altar Society were allowed to do the linens and arrange the flowers.

Being an altar boy was a big deal because you got to come on stage first to light candles and put the big missal on the altar and fill the cruets at the side table with water and wine. Moreover, you went behind the scenes in the sacristy to watch the priest vest, ceremoniously putting on the complicated garments for the ceremony, and, dressed in special garments yourself, to wait for his nod to stride into the sanctuary, tugging the rope of the small bell to announce to the congregation that serious business was about to begin. Unlike the rest of the congregation, you got to speak—even though you were merely parroting the Latin responses—and move around in stylized fashion. On a hot day at a late mass for which you were fasting, you sometimes got to faint like a soldier on parade, which was even better than holding the censer while the priest poured incense onto the hot charcoal. At Communion time, backing ahead of the priest, you got to see an incredible variety of shapes and colors of tongues—pointed to oval, pink to khaki—as the communicants protruded them to receive the host. God must either have had low aesthetic standards or a strong sense of humor, but I always managed to keep a straight face.

Monsignor Roels was technically head of the parish school, which at that time contained all twelve grades in a two-story building a half-block from the church and rectory. Two grades occupied each of the four classrooms downstairs. The high school upstairs had one room for English, one for social sciences, one for typing and shorthand, one for what was called science (the nuns could keep a straight face too), a library, an office, and a large study hall. Since the high school student population was seventy-five in the year I graduated, we were not over-crowded. A sort of half-basement was occupied by a lunchroom, a gym with a stage at one end and balcony at the other and along one side, restrooms, and dressing rooms. Day-to-day operations were left to the ten Sisters of Saint Joseph (Salina motherhouse rather than the more prestigious one in Carondolet): four for the grade school, four for the high school, one to teach music, one to keep house at the convent built next to the school.

Socially as well as doctrinally the school was very stable. My class had seventeen people in it, and I had gone to school with more than half of them since second grade. Billy Stuesse joined us late in grade school when his father was transferred to Cooper County as game warden, and Ray McKinzie's family moved to a nearby farm about the same time. A couple of others joined the freshman class from country schools, three others from New Franklin three miles away. One boy dropped out after eighth grade. One girl had moved away in the middle grades but came back for high school.

There was more social variety than this roll call implies. One girl's father was in prison, having shot the wrong man. One girl's parents were divorced. There was something indefinably or undiscussably odd about the family situation of a third. My father was a Protestant who didn't even go to church. Nobody was ostracized or made to feel inferior for these or any other reasons, but no one felt any obligation to restrict one's circle of friends to the class. The nuns had what we increasingly felt to be really weird beliefs and attitudes, but they weren't snobs, and they valued individual character over family status.

With Monsignor Roels it was a little harder to tell. He wasn't a snob in the sense that he seemed to care about people's family status, and the nuns and everybody else were sufficiently in awe of him that he didn't have to enforce his own status. We rarely saw him except in church, but when he did come down to the school—mostly to the high school, the awfulness of his presence being too much for the grade schoolers to bear—the nuns made it seem like a state visit. He liked to distribute the report cards to the assembled student body, not, since there were only about seventy-five of us, a time-consuming task. Each name would be called, and the student would walk to the front of the room, receive the card and a brief comment on it from the monsignor, and stride or slink back to his or her place.

He seemed to pay special attention to me because he was quite openly weary from years of watching adolescent males reveal their academic inferiority to females, and I was clearly (in his mind—I never bothered to think about it) going to be the first male valedictorian in the history of the school. He was prepared to be indulgent even when, with A's in all my academic subjects, my report card turned up a C in Deportment. (To get lower than a C, you had to hit a nun or desecrate a church or commit whatever an unforgivable sin was.)

Peering at the card over his reading glasses, he said, in an almost jocular tone, "Could it be, Robert, that you are a scholar but not a gentleman? What happened?"

"Well, Father, I guess it was a combination of circumstances." And, unscarred by divine wrath—Monsignor Roels even chuckled a bit—I swaggered back to my seat accompanied by a restrained murmur of astonished approval from my male classmates that I had actually said that and got away with it. We had never suspected that a priest could value cleverness over character.

The nuns, for the most part, couldn't afford to. Even more than the priests, they were responsible for the spiritual welfare of those under their charge; that is, they were supposed to keep us in line with the commandments of God (ten, though we divided differently from the Protestants) and of the Church (six more). But they were also talent scouts for the seminaries and apostolic schools, which trained the next generations of priests and nuns, and they gave us the impression that their status depended on the number of vocations they brought into bloom. Boonville was a tough hustle in this regard, having never, or not within living memory, produced a priest or, except for my sister's brief incursion into the habit, a nun. With me, though any boy who could read without moving his lips was an automatic candidate, they didn't really try—something about my general attitude, perhaps.

I don't know if we ever realized that nuns went to the bathroom—the next question, given the long black habits, would have been "How?"—but we were not sure that they were human. Not all of them seemed to have good sense, like the nun in fifth grade who called me to the front of the room for some malefaction at recess, aimed a backhand blow at my head, and, when I ducked and her knuckles hit the black-board, called me a coward. I was hardly a rebel at that age, but since she was twice my size and knew I wouldn't hit her back, that seemed a singularly stupid analysis.

Sometimes God was good enough to show us a really human side to nuns. In high school, the toughest nun anyone had ever seen—Sister Emily, the English teacher, got more weight behind her slaps, but Sister Caroline had a rougher edge to her tongue, which she used to reproach boys going through the stage of adolescence that involves frequent breaking of wind. (One boy, a year behind me, was notorious for it.) "It's disgusting! You need to exercise some self-control," she would insist. Until, that is, on one of the great days in Catholic education, when she stood at the blackboard writing down a geometry problem and cut one that, we told delighted underclassmen at the first opportunity, almost raised her habit parallel to the floor. That was the last sound for what seemed like ten minutes. She wouldn't turn around, and we didn't dare laugh or look at each other or even make loud choking noises. But we knew what we had heard. And so did she. We never heard that particular lecture again.

Some nuns were human all the time, like Sister Lorena, the six-foot principal who took on the extra work of teaching three of us Algebra II. The other two became engineers. She also taught Latin II, but that was scheduled opposite boys' basketball practice, apparently on the theory that any boy who wanted that much Latin would have already been in a seminary. She was not only a sensible person, but we occasionally got signs that she realized some of her colleagues weren't all that sensible. Like the time when Sister Caroline's replacement, who thought she was tough but was just big, threw my crutches into the hall (maybe I had exploited a basketball injury a little too hard) and ordered me to my seat. "But Sister, I can't walk without my crutches" (logic sometimes baffled them). "Then sit there"—at the back of the room, beside the door.

Part way through the class Sister Lorena walked by, saw the crutches, paused, and motioned to me to come out. I didn't even think about playing the martyr but got up and went to her.

"What are these crutches doing here, Robert?"

"They were thrown out here, Sister."

"Who threw them out, Robert?"

"I don't like to say, Sister."

"Robert . . ."

"Sister Laurentia, Sister."

"Oh." Long pause, and a sigh. "Well, pick them up and go back to class."

Later, a week before the graduation at which I was to give the valedictory address, Sister Laurentia brought me before Sister Lorena demanding that I be expelled from school. I don't remember my particular crime, but all year the senior boys had been working at driving her round the bend, and I had obviously given the last push. Having handed me over to the secular arm, so to speak, she left me with the principal. Sister Lorena looked at me—she was tall even sitting down—and in effect told me to cool it and stay out of Sister Laurentia's way for a while. I almost felt sorry for her because—though she would never have put it this way—she had to put up with Sister Laurentia for at least another year, while I would be free in a week.

Human or not, nuns had killer teaching loads on top of their spiritual duties, they cost incredibly little, and when the supply of nuns ran out in the late 1960s, it became clear that American Catholicism could never again run the way it had for a hundred years or so. They were the shock troops, dealing with the children day to day, cuffing us into shape (sometimes literally—unlike public school teachers, they were not only

allowed but sometimes seemed to feel obligated to go upside our heads)
to deliver to the priest for various rites of passage like first confession
and communion near the end of first grade and confirmation at the age
of twelve. They took us through the questions and answers of the Baltimore Catechism in its progressively longer and more complex versions
that always began with the same question—Who made us?—that any
Catholic born before 1960 can answer in his sleep.

We learned an incredible amount of complicated stuff. Like our
church interiors and our ceremonies, our doctrines were far more complicated than those of the Protestants. We had everything they had and
a lot more besides: limbo and purgatory besides heaven and hell; the
ordinal virtues (prudence, justice, temperance, and fortitude) and the
twelve fruits of the Holy Ghost as well as the cardinal virtues of faith,
hope, and charity (each of which had a separate prayer for acquiring
it). The Protestants had, depending on the height of theological rigor,
as few as two sacraments. We had seven. Three sets of mysteries of the
Blessed Virgin Mary, five to a set. Seven each of corporal and spiritual
works of mercy. Holy days of obligation—to attend mass—in addition
to Sundays.

In fact, a healthy number of students from the Catholic school attended mass every weekday. I certainly did. My father had made
the promises required of a non-Catholic, and whatever he thought of
churches, a contract was a contract. Besides, it occurred to me a lot
later, his Presbyterian heritage made him think that being awake before dawn was virtuous in itself. Weekday masses were shorter—no sermons—and frequently we said a rosary in unison or followed English
translations of the mass in missals of varying thickness and complexity.
You could tell the depth of involvement by the number of colored place-
ribbons the worshipper brought into play. A really serious Catholic
could shift back and forth from "ordinary" (standard) to "proper" (gos-

pel and other prayers for a particular saint's day or season, sometimes with appendages) with the speed and dexterity of a trucker crossing the Rockies.

Most kids didn't go to Communion on weekdays because you had to fast (for the benefit of younger Catholics, that meant no food or drink, including water, after midnight), and piety gave way to common sense. But on the first Friday of each month—if you went to Communion on nine of these in a row, without committing a mortal sin in between or ever afterwards, you earned a Plenary Indulgence or remission of all temporal punishment due to sin, which meant that when you died, you could skip purgatory and go straight to heaven—one school class would be responsible for a school breakfast so that everyone would have the opportunity to take Communion, then breakfast on doughnuts and long johns and cocoa, and, best of all from our point of view, start classes a little later. You knew it was a first Friday when you came into school and found all the drinking fountains covered by inverted buckets so that no one would forget and break the fast.

The rest of the school day was more normal except for catechism class and the monthly distribution of a pious magazine called *Manna* which featured in every issue a story about a very pious child who lived a blameless life and died young. Even to me, credulous if not pious, this seemed like a losing proposition.

But mostly we did what other elementary and high school students did. We had all the subjects required by the state. We had school plays and athletics, though, like the public schools in the outlying towns with whom we formed the Cooper County League, no football, and our coaching, by the man who drove the school bus, was even less serious. We had a band too small to march and a girls' chorus. There had been a boys' and mixed chorus, but one year the nun in charge tried to introduce a medley including "Come to the Church in the Wildwood," during which the baritones sang, on one note, "Oh, come, come, come, come, come, come, come, come." We never got any further than that—sometimes we wouldn't stop—and the boys' chorus was disbanded. But we still sang in the choir.

The school did everything more cheaply and with fewer people than the public school. We didn't have as much to do, but what we did everybody did. You sang in the choir whether you could sing or not. Everyone had a role, backstage or on, in the class plays, and there weren't any auditions because the longest parts went to the fastest and best memorizers. Unless you were totally inept, you played or at least suited up for basketball and softball, girls as well as boys.

The point of all this, or one point, was to convince ourselves and everyone else that despite considerable evidence to the contrary, Catholics were normal Americans. We all knew that Protestants suspected us of a secret loyalty to Rome. I had trouble believing this until, staying with my grandparents in Evansville, I was taken across the Ohio River to Henderson, Kentucky, for an afternoon and met a boy about my age who recounted his father's grievance against the Democratic party for nominating Al Smith, a notorious Catholic, four presidential campaigns earlier and thus forcing him to vote Republican for the only time in his life. I don't remember whether my brief acquaintance believed that Catholics stored arms in church basements and were training the Knights of Columbus as an elite corps in preparation for a coup. I do remember that I said nothing about being a Catholic and felt guilty at missing the opportunity of suffering for my faith.

As a reaction against real or suspected imputations of disloyalty, we Catholics had to prove that we were more American than anybody else, though, given our interpretation of some unfortunate events in the sixteenth century, less Anglophilic. The papal flag was displayed in the sanctuary next to the American flag, or vice versa. We belonged by virtue of baptism to the mystical Body of Christ, encompassing all Catholics living in time and eternity. But we also lived in twentieth-century America.

Catholic education obviously modified that process. We didn't go to school with Protestant kids, and except for neighborhood alliances that tended to weaken as school friendships developed, we didn't play with them all that much. Even in a town as small as Boonville, we hung out in different places. Public school kids went to Boss Hirlinger's confectionery. Nobody tried to make us feel unwelcome there, but I always had the feeling that I was in foreign territory. Catholic school kids, at least the ones I associated with, went to Foster's Drug Store. The Ice Cream Mart was sort of neutral territory, but I started going there and hanging out with non-Catholic kids because we all carried the *Daily News* and that was a convenient place to play the pinball machines and wait for the press run to finish.

We didn't think about this as an economic motive, but in fact we knew that we were going to have to live in an economy dominated by non-Catholics. We knew the names of the businessmen who belonged to "our Church," but they were held up as models rather than as people we were expected to patronize. Leo Kempf and Alfred Lammers were Catholics and barbers; Bill Robinson wasn't. I didn't go to Bill, even though he was my father's friend for fifty years and I found him a lot more interesting than the other two, fathers of schoolmates, because he adjusted my head to his convenience rather than my comfort, not because he wasn't a Catholic. Glover's Men's Store was owned by a non-Catholic; Brownsberger's by a Catholic. Squinch Waldersheid (no one used his real first name, Herman) was a Catholic druggist; Frank Foster wasn't. Where you went depended on personal taste, not religious affiliation.

Anyway, that's the way it worked in my family. My mother could hardly warn me against associating with Protestants, since she had married the least respectable member of a very respectable Protestant family, or atheists, since her father was vocally anticlerical. After Grandpa and Mom were dead, Dad confessed that he would tell the old man that he was thinking of joining the Catholic Church just to hear him sputter—which he did better than anyone I had ever heard. So it was complicated. Morally, Dad was more upright than most Catholics, most of the time, and when he wasn't he seemed to feel worse about it than they did. Intellectually and aesthetically, my grandfather was a lot more interesting than anyone else I knew, Catholic or otherwise, except for Monsignor Roels, and Grandpa looked as though he had more fun doing a wider variety of things and was saddled with a lot less responsibility.

In fact, though we didn't know much about Protestant beliefs and practices, we were fascinated by what they didn't have—all the burdens of belief and behavior with which we often felt saddled. We couldn't go to movies during Lent, not because it was a sin but because it would leave us open to social disapproval from Protestants as well as other Catholics. We couldn't go to a whole lot of movies at all because the Legion of Decency disapproved of them, ranking some "objectionable in part for all" (adults and the bolder big kids might go to these) and some "condemned," which no one I knew even thought of seeing. We were asked—in social terms, compelled, since on a designated Sunday everyone in church would know that you were refusing—to take a yearly pledge to follow those recommendations.

Protestants didn't get out of school on our holy days, but then they didn't have to go to church on those days, and it wasn't specifically a sin for them not to go to church on a Sunday if it was grossly inconvenient. True, the Catholic Church was more tolerant of drinking, (modest) dancing, and gambling, but Protestants had a lot more latitude in dealing with the opposite sex.

We realized that we knew a lot that Protestant kids didn't—dogmas, doctrines, and so on—and more vaguely felt that we were part of a long and noble tradition in which they did not share. But they seemed indifferent to our knowledge, and they seemed to know and to put into practice a lot of things, mostly about sex and dancing and secular institutions, of which we were ignorant and which came to seem a lot more attractive.

We had heard over and over again in the gospel the parable of the unjust steward who decides to make friends with the Mammon of wickedness because, the moral clearly stated, "No man can serve two masters." But culturally and socially speaking, that was what all of us Catholic kids seemed to be expected to do: form good marriages without any knowledge or experience of sex; be independent adults after a rigid doctrinaire training; succeed in a modern, secular world with a medieval religious training watered down by lower-class nineteenth-century piety.

Oddly enough, most of us not only survived that experience but have even thrived in a fashion that our parents would not consider at all modest. More of the class of 1951 went to college than any previous class, and the trend continued. Perhaps the low birth rate of the mid-thirties meant that our families had fewer children to raise. Maybe postwar prosperity affected everyone, regardless of race or religion. So the academic education we got served us well enough.

The religious training seemed to leave an outward and visible sign like an old-fashioned smallpox vaccination, though less well in my family than in most others. I got a medal for having the highest grades in religion over four years of high school, went to Catholic schools between kindergarten and graduate school, and even taught in a Catholic university. My mother used to worry that if I got too far from home and too highly educated and married someone unsuitable, I might stop going to church. She was right, but my sister the nun beat me out of the fold. She left not only the Sisters of Saint Joseph but, after getting into a hassle over Christian education with a priest who decided that he was infallible, the Church altogether to be elected the lay moderator of the Evangelical Church (higher church than it sounds) in Missouri. My brother is still a pillar of the St. Peter and Paul's parish in Boonville, though as a member of the church council he opposed head-on a pastor with his own ideas of infallibility.

The three of us don't bother to discuss religion. I sometimes feel that I didn't leave the Church; it left me. The physical church of my childhood, semigothic, with a linear focus on a decorated plaster altar reaching almost to the high ceiling at the east end, toward Jerusalem, has been torn down. It has been replaced by a structure looking from the outside like something run up by Congregationalists and inside like a fan-shaped auditorium focused on a low table in the southeast. The doctrinal church I grew up in would have excommunicated me on at least two counts. The last time I spoke to a priest, he said that I should not feel isolated because of my status. I forebore from saying that I didn't want to belong to a church that would have me, and in fact I realized that for a long time, even when outwardly I was behaving most piously, I had felt isolated not from the idea of the Church but from the priests and congregations in the parishes to which I had belonged. Anyway, the Church I knew was founded not upon Peter the Rock or even on Monsignor Roels but on the Sisters of St. Joseph. And there aren't enough of them to go around anymore.

Is anything left? Besides the physical structure of my childhood church, most of the outward and visible signs of inward and spiritual grace that we were taught to recognize have disappeared. Instead, there's a whole cottage industry producing humor about being brought up Catholic, and a lot of funny-comic and funny-weird things did happen. Thinking about some of the beliefs and practices I followed, I am not exactly ashamed of them, but I wouldn't tell anyone about them because they wouldn't understand. But they aren't that funny to me. Besides, what better doctrines were offered then? The views that life can be ordered and that one has some control over one's behavior and destiny may be illusory, but as operative illusions they beat many of the alternatives. So do beliefs that you are inevitably part of a larger body and that the material world does not encompass the whole of experience.

Many years later, I discovered that Protestants could share these views. In fact, after a long committee meeting in which academic liberal humanists wrung their hands, refusing to come to a decision between two difficult alternatives, I was relieved to find a colleague who was also a Southern Baptist minister and could follow a hard train of reasoning to an unpalatable end. We didn't talk quite the same language, but we spoke mutually intelligible dialects.

On the other hand, it was a shock to visit a few years ago the Santuario at Chimayo, New Mexico, a shrine complete with holy mud from a hole quite openly restocked by the priests and votive offerings of crutches and doll limbs, with a woman I had felt very close to. She turned out to be the ultimate protestant with a small *p*, reacting in shock and indignation against popery and the exploitation of Hispanic peasant superstition. And I realized that, at a very deep level, I had more in common with the people she pitied and wanted to enlighten. I could see some point in being a Catholic that the American church and its followers seemed to have forgotten. But it wasn't really my point any more.

Grandfather Murray, late 1930s

The author's father, circa 1929

The author's parents, circa 1939

The author in the country, circa 1937

The author, circa 1937

The author, his father, and his brother, John, 1940

The author, late grade school

The Davis family home

The cattle chute

*The author's sister with pet chicken
and Buttons the dog*

*The author (right), his father, and John,
circa 1941*

Saints Peter and Paul School
(Courtesy of Saints Peter and Paul School)

Monsignor Roels, pastor of Saints Peter
and Paul parish, early 1950s

The sanctuary of the old Catholic church

*John's first Communion and the author
as altar boy, circa 1947*

*Boys softball team, Boonville Catholic
High School, 1950. The author is in
the back row, sixth from left.
(Courtesy of Saints Peter and Paul School)*

*The author dressed for a Boonville
American Legion baseball game*

Town and Country

When I tell people that I milked cows and raised hogs and bucked bales when I was a kid, they assume that I grew up on a farm. (Perhaps I picked up my grandfather's habit of exaggeration so that the stories sound like the grimmer passages in Hamlin Garland.) But I didn't: there was as big a gulf between me and the country kids as there was between me and the public school kids, the black kids, or the grown-ups. You were either town or country, and there wasn't any overlap. My mother was a little rabid on the distinction, but her attitude was extreme, not unique.

My father had a recurring dream of living on a farm. Perhaps because my mother not only refused to move to the country but didn't even like to hear about the country, he mentioned it only when necessity overcame prudence. As a child, he had lived in both town and country, and perhaps he figured that he could be a better farmer than his mother, who had a lot of interesting theories picked up from reading or invented herself that were hard to translate into practice. Outdoing his father was no problem, since Grandpa Davis showed no interest in farming or anything else but his sets of nineteenth-century English novels, which may explain Dad's distress at my obsessive reading.

During the war, he apprenticed himself to Old Man Darby, or Gene, as opposed to his son, Baby Gene, who traded in farm property. For a while they owned a farm southwest of town. The house seemed to me cramped and barren, but there was a spring that seemed marvelous, and once I was allowed to go with a large group of men and boys to chop down a bee tree and collect the honey. The best part was watching grown men run like kids when the tree crashed and the bees swarmed out. Dad also took me with him hunting—I had trouble keeping up— and fishing on the Petit Saline Creek which ran through the property, and I found that boring.

I don't know that Mom had lived in the country as a child, since she could have ridden horses as a town girl, but either her experience or her prejudice convinced her that she didn't want to. I think that she refused even to drive out to the farm. It took two of the strongest forces in her lifetime, the Depression and the Second World War, to get her away from street lights and concrete.

I could vaguely remember the time during the Depression—1937?— when we had lived on a farm in Morgan County, somewhere between my grandparents near Florence and my aunt and uncle's chicken farm on the edge of Otterville. When I was taken into Sedalia to visit my aunt in the hospital, I backed away from a toilet because it had water in it, like Ruthie and Winfield Joad in *The Grapes of Wrath*. A few photos survive: Dad in the kind of bib overalls he never again wore; Mom in a dress, looking as if she had been set down bodily in the yard and was waiting to be picked up and put back on concrete, as God had intended; me dressed carefully in a kind of sailor outfit, complete with hat, posed with a flower, like a charm to guide me out of this underworld.

Before we moved there from western Kansas, I suffered from a severe rash that no doctor could diagnose. One day Dad mentioned this to a client—he was selling dime-a-week burial insurance door to door— a black woman with a lot of children. She advised him to buy a milk goat and take me off cows' milk. It worked. I don't know if we moved to the farm because of the allergy or even if we had the goat in Morgan County. Wherever it was, Mom hated that goat almost as much as she hated cats or anything else as independent as she was. She never tried to make me feel that the improvement in my health was less important than the annoyance of milking what she invariably called, as if the initials were the name of a breed, "that g.d. goat," but I had the impression that it was a near thing and I'd better not push it.

I don't know how long we lived there, but it was too long for Mom. Years later my father, in an uncharacteristic reminiscent mode, talked almost enthusiastically about the hard times and tough people he had known in the Ozark foothills. "But then," he added, "your mother got to chewing on me so hard that I went down to Coffeyville and got a job selling lessons [I forget what kind] door to door."

Mom didn't care what Dad sold as long as the doors were close together, and in our first years in Boonville, she seemed perfectly happy to be married to the owner of a pool hall. But the war came along, and that occupation didn't seem very patriotic or even, for a man nearing thirty-four with two children to support, very prudent. So he got a job as brakeman on the Katy for the duration. For a while, that was all he did—though railroad men worked almost incessantly during the war—and then, for reasons I never thought to ask about while Mom and Dad were alive, we moved three miles west of town to the Big Bend restaurant, gas station, and tourist cabins.

If there was one thing Mom hated more than the country, it was the restaurant business, which she labeled "the hardest way of serving the Lord there is." But at least, though we were definitely outside of town, we weren't really in the country. The business sat right beside Highway 40, and even with the traffic reduced by gasoline and tire rationing, we probably saw more people than we did on a normal day in town, more, I imagined, than a farming family saw in weeks at a time.

Except for the fact that there was no one to play with but my younger brother, still one of the littler little kids, it was a pretty good place for a kid. Out back was a small pond with frogs to listen to and startle into jumping and some small willows overhanging the water which formed a refuge when I needed to nurse real or imagined psychic wounds or just to daydream. Between the cabins and the Katy railroad line was a slope abandoned to a kind of plant that looked like a cross between a scrub tree and a weed and which was gratifyingly easy to break off but useless thereafter.

If there was no one to play with, there were plenty of people to talk to, or, since I was a kid, to listen to. Our living quarters were in the main building, so if I got bored, all I had to do was come into the restaurant and listen to the customers and delivery men or go into the gas station office and talk to Johnmeyer—his last name—who walked with a rocking motion on a built-up shoe to compensate for his damaged leg, which kept him out of the war. He was cheerful or tolerant with me in a country-shrewd way that even then I didn't put much stock in. One of the songs on the juke box, "There's a Star-Spangled Banner Waving Somewhere," contained a plea to be allowed to fight in the war, "never mind my crippled laig." (The other one played incessantly was Duke Ellington's "Don't Get Around Much Anymore," which to my ear began, "MIS-TER Saturday Dance.") Johnmeyer seemed to have no regrets about his noncombatant status.

One recurrent and memorable visitor was Zeke, the dead animal man, who collected raw material for the rendering plant farther west. My brother was fascinated by Zeke and named his imaginary friend after him. I had been less enterprising and denied models: my imaginary friend in Kansas had been named Pal.

The livestock auction barn a few hundred yards to the west smelled different from Zeke and his truck, though not necessarily better, and it offered a lot more variety. Twice every week farmers and feeders would congregate in clusters in the concrete halls or on the wooden bleachers overlooking the auction ring, most of them carrying canes to poke cattle or thwack hogs and sheep in the right direction or just to lean on. Mules were still important enough to have a separate sale day, and they had far more distinctive personalities than the other livestock. I didn't learn much about the respective merits of the stock driven through the arena because I wasn't interested enough to watch very closely or listen to the sellers and bidders talk. But I was interested in the styles of the various auctioneers. Colonel Patrick, the title honorary, wasn't as fast as his son R.D., but he had a brassy timbre to his voice which I admired, and he and his son were the center of attention. But unlike my brother and one of my classmates who later went to auction school but never practiced professionally, I never wanted to star in this particular show, let alone have a supporting role as one of the farmers.

As I have said, I thought that everybody was different from me and that adults were almost a different species, but the farmers seemed to me especially alien—not inferior, just different. I couldn't imagine becoming like my father, but it seemed even less possible that I would be like one of these people because they moved and sounded too different and their horizons seemed far narrower than those of the Davises and Murrays. During his later years, my father acquired some of the local patina, but at that time he looked leaner, moved more gracefully, and talked less and more circumspectly and with an accent more clipped than any of these people.

It wasn't just because the farmers were adults and therefore alien. After we had lived at Big Bend a while, a family with two children roughly my age moved into the farmhouse across the highway. I could see that I was different from Franklin and his sister, whose name I can't remember, who were real country kids. They seemed exotic because, while I knew a lot of things from books that they didn't, they had a different kind of knowledge and a daring that made me ashamed of my caution. They talked me into stealing tobacco from the restaurant—first cigarettes (Chesterfields, I think) and then chewing tobacco. We split the plug three ways, and Franklin was tough enough to chew it for more than a couple of minutes. Then he fell down and swallowed the plug. The results were protracted and spectacular enough to cure me of a taste for smokeless tobacco. They had the idea of heading cross-country to see the Missouri River in flood. Franklin got stuck in what we called quicksand, and I felt heroic for pulling him out. We wore out before we even got close to the river and caught modified hell at home for wandering off, though I think that my mother was secretly proud of my enterprise. There was nothing heroic about my action when we were playing in a creek and Franklin got attacked by a leech: his sister and I fled ignominiously. I may have learned from Franklin's disasters that a little caution is not necessarily bad.

One thing I learned about the country was that there was a lot more stuff there, including animals. Franklin discovered two real swords in the attic of his house, and we pretended to fight with them. Fortunately, the only thing we stuck them into was the ceiling. On the other side of the road, someone left with us a raccoon and cage, and my brother and I would watch him try to wash bread before eating it. Someone else gave me a set of traps which I set in the nearby creeks, trying to feel like Daniel Boone. I never caught anything and, in fact on Christmas Day of what must have been 1943, felt ashamed of myself and gathered them up. But I did learn something about moving through the countryside. Some things were benign, such as the battered Scottie dog who turned up at the door and made a pleasant companion until he was run over. Some things were treacherous, like the big bucket of tar that in the morning was solid and later in the day, as I discovered when I put my foot on it again, was not. That incident ruined a shoe, more serious in the days of rationing than now, but it gave my brother

one of the oldest stories in his repertory. Even more treacherous was
the large cat who turned up. I begged Mom to let it stay, and against all
her instincts, for she hated cats, she gave in. But then the cat jumped
on the table and grabbed a piece of steak off a platter, and I can still
remember seeing the screen door jerk open and the cat exit at the end
of Mom's toe.

I was like the country kids in one way: I commuted. We called it
taking the school bus, and it set us off from the town kids. The schedule was inexorable, and missing the school bus was a catastrophe or a
crime, depending upon the cause. The meanest nuns hesitated to keep
country kids after school. If a country kid was kept in, town kids felt a
little like a gaggle of jaywalkers in the company of a major felon, and
even the toughest country kid was a little subdued by this punishment.

The school bus had its own kind of social interaction, based on the
route. The first to board established territories by saving seats (like
church, the older you got, the farther back you went, as far away as
you could get from the contamination of adult supervision). Groups assembled on the way in and dispersed on the way out. But despite the
segregation by age and clique, there was no real privacy because everyone was jammed together, and there was—until the bus was almost
empty—no leisure because the pent-up energy made all activities, male
anyway, a muted form of grab-ass with the object, barely concealed
by the atmosphere of hilarity, of establishing and maintaining pecking
orders. Details of these rides have faded, but I retain the impression of
jostling and noise.

Even riding the bus didn't make me a country kid in anyone's mind,
including mine. I rode with the ones on my route who went to the
Catholic school, and I played with the ones across the street who didn't.
But I was not like them. For one thing, it was clear in all kinds of subtle
ways of speaking and acting that I had lived in town before moving

there. Besides, it was obvious to anyone who knew Mom or even looked at her that we were going to move back the minute her piece of the war effort was finished. Even missing the bus was forgivable, since Mom could sympathize with a reluctance to leave town. She couldn't convince the Axis to let us out of Big Bend. But she did get pregnant with my sister late in 1943. That may not have been her only motive (the fact that her children were spaced five years apart seems to make accident unlikely), but it did get us back to town.

Maybe I had gotten older and more observant, or maybe I was just trying to reestablish my own urbanity, but about this time I began to notice that country kids were very different from us. They carried lunch-boxes, for one thing, while Mom gave me money to eat at the counter of Phelps's Drug Store two blocks from school. But they also looked different. Partly it was their hair. Some of the boys had a cereal-bowl look about them, and the girls' hair just looked odd, probably because it was done in the last fashion that their mothers had learned.

Partly it was the clothes. Not jeans or overalls, since they weren't allowed in the Catholic school. (In the sixties, when bib overalls were chic, I doubt that many of us wore them because someone might have thought we were serious about it. But I still dress in jeans on teaching days in belated defiance of the nuns' dress code.) Not even, or at least for school wear, shirts and blouses made out of feed and flour sacks. Or anyway not the sacks with "Pillsbury" across the front. Some sacks had flowered prints on them to ease the transition from barn to closet. (I had a few shirts like that—my mother could sew a lot better than she could cook, though her color sense was my first indication she was fallible.) And of course most people used cloth from bolts to make clothing.

But in those days, *store-bought* was a term of approval whether it applied to clothes or to bread. I was raised to believe that country people made things because they couldn't get to town or couldn't afford to buy them. Town people were fortunate enough to be able to go into a store and pay cash for what they needed. (The back-to-the-earth movement of the sixties was popular mostly with people who had not come from the earth or, even more important, from the Depression, when making your own was a sign of poverty and powerlessness.)

Today, there are still distinctions between town and country kids—"soshes" (or socialites) and "kickers" (or "goat-ropers") when my children were in high school—but now it seems more a matter of choice than of necessity.

During the school year, the bus schedule put the country kids into totally separate social and even spiritual categories. Country kids got to school too late to go to daily mass and had to leave right after school and thus were excused from various religious exercises, including altar boy practice. As a result, even the nuns expected country kids to be less pious than town kids. We town kids envied them this advantage.

But there were various disadvantages to being a country kid. For one thing, even if country kids wanted to suck up to the nuns, they didn't have much opportunity. More as a corollary than as a direct result, they were not expected to be really good students. None of the ones in my class went to college from high school, and only one of them later bootstrapped himself into and through college at all. Socially, at least by town standards, the only standards that really counted as far as I was concerned, they were at a disadvantage because the bus whisked all of them away from secular pleasures. They couldn't hang out at Foster's or Boss Hirlinger's. They couldn't go to the library even if they had wanted to. They couldn't go to the movies as often as we did, and in the summer, like the black kids, they couldn't go to the swimming pool. They did have ponds, but those had inconvenient features like mud and snakes, always assumed to be water moccasins.

On the other hand, the boys seemed to have fewer fights on the playground, probably because they were less prone to the kind of posturing that caused fights, and the ones they had were a lot shorter because they were not only tougher but, put to work early, they were a lot stronger. And they grew up faster than we did in a lot of other ways. The boys smoked earlier, oftener, and more openly than we did. When we were still trying to get high on Virginia Dare bar sour, they were drinking real alcohol—three of them killed a bottle of wine on the bus heading to a junior high basketball game in Bunceton, and since all three were starters, we lost even worse than we were going to anyway and not just because I was put in as substitute in my first organized game.

The first girl in our class to use make-up, or maybe the first girl to seem sexually mature enough to tease openly, was from the country. Whether because of her boldness, my immaturity, or her country origins, I was repelled as much as I was attracted. I don't want to malign anybody either way, but I am pretty sure that all four of the town boys in my class were virgins when they graduated and that at least three-fourths of the country boys were not.

Country kids—boys anyway—had access to cars, money, and certain kinds of adult skill and knowledge long before we did. They seemed to go from kids to grown-ups with almost no intervening stage. Some of them were smart as well as shrewd. Donald Vollmer was so smart that I don't think anyone, except me and maybe the principal of the school, who taught the two of us and Jerry Lammers an overload course in Algebra II, knew just how smart he was. That was the only time in my life, except in grade school penmanship, that I have been at the bottom of a class. In neither case did I envy skills that I obviously didn't have. In other subjects Donald didn't do as well, but he had far greater social skills than I.

Maybe this was because he and other country kids spent more time with adults than we did or because, with less leisure, they learned to take their pleasures straighter and faster. The other town kids and I respected their maturity, but none of my group tried to imitate it. For one thing, though we had trouble imagining the way in which they lived, we could see that it had a lot of disadvantages.

I could see it better than some because I had a better vantage point than the other town kids. A couple of years after the war my parents achieved a compromise both could accept. They bought "the old Effinger place" on the ridge at the east edge of town. Like most small towns, Boonville didn't have suburbs, but it did, and does, sort of bleed out into the country at the edges, and there are transition areas where the land isn't built up but the acreage remaining is too small to be called or thought of as a farm by anyone who knows about farms. In local terms, what is left isn't a lot, and it isn't a farm. It is a place.

The two-story brick house showed the seams where successive additions had been made in the course of almost a century, furnished with six fireplaces, a wine cellar, and a dirt-floored basement where, supposedly, slaves had been housed. There were various outbuildings: two barns, two chickenhouses, a smokehouse, two garages, an equipment shed, and an outhouse that wasn't used but could be if you felt inclined. (Its site later became a very rich flower-bed.) For a while, the only heat came from the one remaining functional fireplace in the living room, the gas stove in the dining room, and a huge black wood-burning cook-stove in the kitchen. The upstairs had no heat until after I went away to college. I found a collection of old bottles in the basement, and, in one of the upstairs closets, piles of dusty old magazines in German. Outside, twenty-six acres left from the original farm sloped down to the Training School dairy farm to the east and down to a deeply eroded ravine and pond and up the other side on the south. The land just behind the house was fenced for orchards or for small holding lots for various kinds of animals except for the big back yard, with a circular drive, where everybody parked. It had an impressively thick front door that nobody used because everyone came through the back door into the kitchen.

It certainly felt like the country in this and other ways. Dad could plant a huge garden and raise chickens and keep a milk cow for our table and there was room to pen or pasture livestock—mostly cattle, some hogs, and once some sheep—for him to trade. When we first moved there—I had lived very close to the main highway and trucks shifting gears day and night for almost five years—I would wake up in the night and think, What was that? It would be nothing at all. You could look out the back door and see several ridges across to still higher ground, a distant farmhouse the only visible dwelling.

Beyond that, in Mom's terms and to a great extent in mine, lay the heart of an immense darkness, the real country, where along dirt roads, which choked you with dust if a car had passed in the last fifteen minutes or mired you in mud or slammed you against the car roof with the ruts and holes, boxy houses stood in a little patch of trees and a complex of buildings full of tangled and mysterious strings and strips of metal and you had to walk through globs of chicken shit in the back yard, where the only lights were inside the house and barn, with perhaps one on a pole in the yard, and the newspaper was delivered, if at all, a day late and the only other thing to read was a back issue of *Missouri Farmer* or *Country Gentleman* or a nineteenth-century textbook whose cover looked like a field after a prolonged drought. Worst of all, the country seemed to Mom and thus to me a place where there was nobody to talk to, day in and day out, except on shopping Saturdays and church Sundays.

Fortunately for Mom, and maybe even more fortunately for Dad, across the big lawn from the front door there was a paved highway that led to town, at most a mile and a half away. We might get our mail in a box by the side of the road—for a long time our address was Rural Route 1—but there was also a streetlight, we had city water, gas, and electricity, and Mom didn't have to weed anything or feed anything with four legs or feathers except, if she felt like it, the dogs, who in any case ate leftovers. Or milk anything at all.

So I wasn't a country kid. I didn't ride a bus, and if I hurried I could come home for lunch instead of carrying a lunch-box (this was before the Catholic school got a hot-lunch program). I was big enough to go anywhere I wanted during my free daylight hours, and before too long I was big enough to go out at night.

But I did get an inkling of what it was like to be a country kid. I learned to chop wood. I learned how to cut grass, first with a reel mower and then with a rotary power mower that whanged off the exposed roots of the old trees in the front yard. It seemed to me that every time I finished mowing the last patch it was time to start again on the first patch. And there was more to mow every year as another fence between lawn and farm area came down, until I escaped to college and Dad bought a tractor. (My brother insists that the tractor came after he went to college, but I don't believe it. He always got off easier.) I learned to push a hand cultivator what seemed like miles through the rich black dirt of the garden where we raised enough potatoes to last through the winter. I learned how to tell when vegetables are ripe. I learned how to assemble, run, and clean a cream separator and—it didn't take skill, only muscle and persistence, innate or outwardly induced—how to operate a hand-cranked butter churn.

I learned where food came from. We raised chickens, mostly for food, laying hens being too much trouble and eggs cheap enough anyway. That means they had to be killed first. Mostly we cut off their heads with a hatchet, but more experienced grown-ups would grab a chicken just below the head and whirl the body around until the head came off.

Whichever method was used, the headless chicken would run around—
"like a chicken with its head chopped off" is a proverbial expression
for mindless panic, but it means more if you have seen it acted out—
until it fell over and lay there twitching. My grandmother, probably
the gentlest person I have ever known, killed chickens as a matter of
course. This may sound disgusting to townspeople, but it isn't as bad as
plucking a chicken, and that in turn isn't as bad as the smell of feathers
scalded in hot water to make the plucking easier.

People raised this way are not likely to have scruples about hunting
because a gunshot is quicker and cleaner. We didn't shoot chickens,
not just because ammunition cost money but because the lead made
for difficult chewing. It's rather surprising to realize that most people
I know today have never killed anything on purpose except bugs, or at
least not anything they planned to eat.

This fact of life gave country people a certain detachment from the
animal kingdom. You might not kill and eat the cattle and hogs you
raised, but you knew what was going to happen to them. You might
even get fond of them. The runt pig of one of our litters was too small
to compete for food, so we brought him up to the house and fed him
with a bottle until he was big enough for solid food. He lived in the
doghouse under the precast concrete steps, and when the back door
opened would rush out, snorting a greeting. But there was no question that he was a pig, not a funny-looking dog, and when he got big
enough, back he went to the barnyard to share his siblings' fate. My
sister made a pet of a chicken, but that didn't save it from getting the
chop or taking that last Ferris wheel ride.

So I didn't entirely escape the influence of the country, and I can still
chop wood and walk through the woods without getting all scratched
up or a pasture without stumbling into a cow patty. Probably I could
kill a chicken if I really had to, though I'm a little vague about how to
pluck and gut it.

But I would never have made a country boy. I rather liked the pigs for their character and intelligence; they reminded me of my grandfather snorting about something. On the whole they weren't much trouble. Young pigs had to be vaccinated and some castrated, and that was a struggle, but it gave me a chance to show off my growing strength— and better them than me. Once, however, Grandpa and Dad both had to leave the place while one of the sows was expected to farrow a lit- ter, and I was left in charge. "All you have to do," Grandpa said, "is watch and see if the pigs are coming out all right. If one gets stuck, just reach inside the sow, turn it around, and help it out." If I had ever had any illusions that I would make a farmer, this killed them. Fortunately, labor didn't start until after an adult returned to take charge.

Chickens, on the other hand, were just boring, and a whole lot of chickens, like the ones I saw at my aunt and uncle's commercial chicken farm before they moved into town, were exponentially more boring than a few chickens. Sheep are sometimes too stupid to recog- nize their own lambs, which in our case seemed invariably to be born during the middle of a sleet storm. The various pastoral images in the Bible still seem ludicrous to me. Cows, at least milk cows, were like a ball and chain. You couldn't go away and leave them, and they were damned uncomfortable to be around because they had to be found and driven in and milked and cleaned up after. I had stopped being allergic to the milk; in fact, in my mid-teens I drank a gallon a day, but that didn't make me any fonder of the source.

Dad was shrewd enough to realize that my attitude toward the coun- try was more like Mom's than it was like his. He was also grown-up enough to think that it didn't matter. And optimist enough to think that the proper exposure would convert me. He assigned me the milk- ing chores, which I made tolerable only by trying to imitate popular singers of the day like Bing Crosby and later Mel Tormé. Occasionally he would grumble about an output lower than anticipated, which put the cow under greater pressure than me—if she was responsible, she went to the butcher. I just had to listen to Dad. On these occasions, he would come down to the barn to study my milking technique and try to correct it.

Dad was a fantastic milker. The volume and pressure he produced made the foam rise high above the liquid, and the barn cats would stand ten feet away waiting for a well-directed squirt. The only reason I could bear to watch him was that I regarded milking as a skill like penmanship or algebra that clearly I was never going to master and was going to find a way to avoid in later life.

But Dad was a stubborn man, and he kept trying to teach me. One evening he came down as I was driving the Jersey cow into her stall and getting ready for what both of us regarded as an ordeal.

"I'm going to show you how to milk the right way," he said. "You've got to be gentle with the cow."

He took the bucket, swung it between his legs and the stool made of two pieces of two-by-four nailed in a T beneath his backside, tucked the cow's somewhat matted tail between the outside of his knee and the inside of hers, and began his virtuoso milking performance. The cats and I watched, expectantly or reluctantly as our natures dictated. All of a sudden the cow worked her tail loose and hit Dad upside the head with a brush full of half-dried cow shit and kicked the bucket from between his legs. Without even stopping to swear, he rocked back on the stool for momentum and forward with a right jab to the ribs that sounded like a bass drum note. The cow staggered and bounced off the partition and stood there trembling.

I don't know if I had the guts actually to say, "I think I've got it, Dad. Be gentle with the cow." But I certainly thought it, and I really didn't have to say it. That was the last milking lesson I ever had, and before long I was released to begin a career "readin' those damned books."

Years later I consulted an allergist—not for milk, but, as part of my inheritance from Grandpa Murray, for almost everything else— who knew where I lived and what I did for a living. He went rapidly through the results of various tests, but he stopped at one line and looked puzzled. "Were you ever around chickens?" Clearly he thought, from looking at me, that something was wrong with his lab work. It took me a minute to remember cleaning out our chickenhouse and my visits to the chicken farm. I wasn't sorry to remember this from a safe distance, and I was really pleased that, except for deep in my lungs, I didn't look a thing like a farm kid.

I was glad to get away even from the edge of the country, and I do not regret it now. But I realized even then and more clearly while writing this that I learned something my children and even my nieces and nephews didn't and couldn't. That was the experience of seeing my parents struggle to build something. In the first seventeen years of their marriage, they had never owned a house, and in our first eight years in Boonville we had lived in five different places. So when they scraped together enough for a down payment on the house and acreage at the edge of town, it was not just the old Effinger place or a place, it was the Place. And it was worth whatever discomfort or inconvenience it took.

And it took a lot. It was an old house, and it had been neglected for a long time. Mom and Dad stretched to the limit to get the place, and for a while we were the only people I knew who rented out rooms inside the basic family dwelling. I regretted that the old bathroom had to be converted to a kitchen because that meant that the mural, not wallpaper but original painting with a pastoral motif, had to be painted over and the end of the hall stretching from front door to back porch enclosed for the new bathroom. But it was rather like camping out.

And it was damned cold in the unheated upstairs, but that made the kitchen stove, just beginning to glow in the morning, all the more comforting, and it certainly brought the family together. The floorboards were splintered and ugly, but when Dad went over them with a rented sander, they turned out to be hardwood. Under the many coats of ugly paint, the banister post and rail were walnut. Nobody I knew had a window on an inside wall but us because the rooms to the south were an addition to the original structure and the second-floor window was left untouched. The living room floor slanted several inches from one side to the other, and Dad discovered that the central beam beneath was rotted through. With jacks, sweat, and half-voiced profanity, he replaced it, and the new beam was like a sign that we were there to stay. (Later, when he put a concrete floor in that part of the basement, the beam made an impression on the males in the family because it was less than six feet from the floor and all of us were taller than that. I can still put my finger on the place where it hit me.)

I don't remember that Dad said anything about the symbolic import of the beam, but later, putting creosote to prevent rot at the bottom of a gatepost before planting it, he said, with mingled satisfaction and melancholy, "That'll make it last long after I'm gone." It didn't, but that was only because we stopped keeping cattle in the front yard and didn't need the gate anymore.

The size and spaciousness of the house and outbuildings impressed me, and those may be the source of my recurring dream of finding previously unsuspected rooms in a familiar house. I've been told that this is a sign of an optimistic and confident outlook on life, an interpretation that at first came as a surprise to me.

Even the garden, which caused me a lot of sweat and annoyance, was a sign of family unity. For one thing, the produce went directly to the table, and I knew that I was making a contribution. For another, the family sometimes worked together. Once, when the potato crop was ready to harvest, Dad decided that it would be easier to hire someone to turn over the rows with a plow than to dig hill by hill. The flaw in this reasoning was that the plow then covered the potatoes again, leaving nothing above ground to show where to dig. So the whole family, including Mom for the only time I can remember, and the dogs, turned out to rescue the crop. The dogs and my little sister were so enthusiastic about digging that the chore turned into a game. I think that this was the only time we planted a garden this big. Either Dad was disillusioned by the result of his labor-saving scheme or we had more money, or both.

About this time Grandpa and Grandma Murray moved from Indiana to live in the downstairs rooms across the hall from the living and dining rooms while Grandpa converted the carriage house across the back yard into a place to live. Now we weren't just an offshoot of the Davises; we were a clan in our own right. Our place wasn't like any other place, and our family wasn't like any other family.

All of the elm trees and some of the others as well as many of those people have died, but the Place is still in the family, and my son goes there every chance he gets. My sister continues to tear out this and shore up that and has done the paperwork to get it declared a historic place. The rest of us are pleased, but we think that it is historic not because the house was built in 1859 but because it belongs to us. Her husband even likes to cut the grass.

Food and Drink

Boonville cuisine was so limited that I did not realize until some time after I left home just how poor a cook my mother was. I'm not maligning her memory. She told her first daughter-in-law that if her husband ever said that she didn't cook as well as Mom, he was lying. In fact, she worked hard at not being a good cook because— and this was long before I had heard of Freud or even of psychology— in this and other ways she was rebelling against her mother, a very good cook in the old German fashion. Fortunately, Mom realized that she was a better bookkeeper than cook and had the sense to use her real talents and hire a housekeeper who was a good cook. A little later, after my grandparents moved just across the big back yard from us, Grandma would practically beg me to eat without any hinting on my part. Even when Mom couldn't get out of cooking, she never poisoned us, and it was obvious then and even more obvious today that none of her children ever suffered from malnutrition. But she didn't spend a lot of time thinking about food. For one thing, I seem to remember that, when asked what he wanted for dinner, Dad would always reply, "Meat, potatoes, and gravy." But this could very well be a memory from the racial, or anyway regional, unconscious, because that was what everybody wanted.

For another thing, there wasn't a hell of a lot more to think about. Trying to describe late 1940s food to my children is largely a process of negation. There was no pizza. There was no Mexican food, though Mom fixed something she called. Spanish rice. I think there was some canned Chinese food, but I can't be sure. The only seafood came in cans, and if you wanted fresh fish, you either had to catch it yourself or know someone who did. Frozen vegetables began to come in toward the end of the period, and TV dinners a little later than that. I ate my first oyster in my mid-thirties, and I can't even guess how old I was when I saw my first bagel. There was no such thing as health food—sprouts would have been regarded as a sign of advanced and poisonous decay.

Somewhere in the United States, even at that point, people were familiar with some of these things, but smalltown middle America, or at least middle Missouri, had no ethnicity. We had a lot of people of German descent, but after a hundred years away from the Old Country and two world wars, they were not inclined to emphasize the connection, so everybody ate white bread from Trout's Holsum Bakery or something else exactly like it. We had plenty of black people, but chitterlings didn't sound very appetizing, and greens reminded the older generation too much of the Depression. The term "soul food" had not been invented to make them sound better.

In fact, we thought that we ate better than people in cities, and considering the Depression and then wartime rationing, we probably did. Near the end of the war, an assistant priest in our parish arranged for his brother, assistant in a Kansas City parish, to bring a grade school basketball team down to play us. We envied the boys their skill and sophistication, but at the meal after the game, we watched them gape at the piles of food and eat straight off the knife butter they had never before seen.

We made up in quantity what we lacked in variety. "Lots of good, solid food" was a powerful charm. And no one had far to go to get it. There were a lot of grocery stores named after their owners—Hopkins', Bantrup's, Blanck's—but for a long time only one supermarket,

the A&P, which I liked because you could feel the coffee beans lump-
ing into the sack, put them in the big red mill with the lever indicating
degrees of fineness in the grinding, smell them as they ground, and
hear the very satisfying noise—thus satisfying all senses but taste, and
at that time I didn't care about that. Even the A&P wasn't very big,
and it didn't have a large stock of the relatively few items it kept on
hand: canned goods; flour and sugar; incredible amounts of Crisco; few
spices. (Early in my marriage, my wife acquired two Spice Islands racks
and filled them. A friend used to visit and stand by the racks, opening
and sniffing one bottle after another. Clearly he came from the same
kind of background.) The stores stocked few prepared or packaged
goods, except for Kraft Macaroni dinners. A dairy case and a freezer
miniscule by contemporary standards held two or three flavors of ice
cream and a little recreational food like Popsicles and Fudgesicles. The
small produce section contained mostly seasonal or the less perishable
items. Every store had a butcher at the back, his apron often stained,
who cut your meat to order, wrapped it in white paper, and tied it with
string pulled from a conical ball and snapped.

But the really interesting food didn't come from stores. The best vegetables and melons came from gardens; the Place and many real farms
had fruit trees and even small orchards. There were a few domestic
berry patches, but most people would rather pick wild ones, especially
blackberries.

In my family and a good many others, buying meat from the store
was a confession of lack of culinary as well as economic foresight. Some
people hunted, but this was before deer had made a comeback in mid-
Missouri, and it took a lot of small game to feed a family. Dad could
hunt, but he probably didn't think the payout worth the effort. However,
area farmers raised a lot of corn, and some of that corn went into steers
being finish-fed for the Kansas City stockyards, so why pay round-trip

fare to the city and back for livestock? (Meat did not exactly equal beef, but it would have scored nearly 100 percent on a word association test.) Many families ate beef from steers that our fathers had actually seen walking around or that we had fed ourselves. Once I even helped my father kill and butcher a young steer. The process wasn't disturbingly yucky because Dad was so unexpectedly skilled that there wasn't much mess and because the process seemed coherent and sensible.

So while you could buy meat at the grocery store, many people in Boonville rented cold storage lockers and bought sides or quarters of beef to be cut up and packaged. If you didn't need a whole beef, you would call around to family and friends, until you got your share down to reasonable proportions. These conversations—many over the phone—had almost a ritual quality: "Bill? Say, I've got a chance to get a side of beef from McKenzie. (Pause.) A half-Angus steer, about two years old. (Pause.) It'll dress out at about 150 pounds a quarter. (Pause.) About 65 cents a pound. (Pause.) Yeah, that's ready to go in the locker. (Pause.) Well, you ask Iva and let me know by this evening." (Evening, in local dialect, was any time after dinner, which was at noon.) This still goes on. My brother once sold five sides of two beeves.

Going to the locker was an adventure because, in the summers before air conditioning, it was the only really cool place in Boonville. Besides, the sight of all that meat, wrapped neatly in white butcher paper labeled with the name of the cut, gave everyone who looked into the locker a sense that the family stood on a solid basis. You couldn't go look at money in the bank, but the beef was right there in front of you. And kids got to help take it out and even to choose what they wanted to eat. When you could see all the way to the back of the locker and most of the packages said "hamburger," you knew that dinners were going to get a lot more boring before they got more interesting.

It wasn't actually against the law to put pork in your locker, but I don't think we ever did. Lots of people raised hogs—we did ourselves—but we never butchered one or even had it butchered, and we even had a smokehouse in which we haven't ever lighted a fire in forty-five years. In fact, we didn't eat pork. We ate bacon and sausage and pork chops, but that wasn't pork. Local hams, identified as being from Cooper or Boone County, were a well-known and expensive delicacy that got top billing at organizational banquets and Holt's Cafe. But hams weren't pork. Neither was lamb, but it wasn't lamb either because, though some people raised sheep, nobody ate them. Still, some people had heard of eating lamb, whereas no one could even imagine eating goat meat.

Chicken was an entirely different kettle of fish. I was over thirty when I heard the old Jewish proverb, "When a poor man eats a chicken, one of them is sick." Apparently I hadn't known any poor people, and I certainly never knew a chicken who lived long enough to die a natural death or even to get sick. It was even slightly disgraceful to be acquainted with a chicken old enough to require baking or stewing. It would have been possible to buy turkeys year-round—Bob Peck had a big turkey farm east of town (as well as two very nubile daughters)—but we only ate them at Thanksgiving and Christmas. Roast goose was something in *A Christmas Carol.* Roast duck couldn't be found even in literature. A few people raised guineas, who made a wheepling noise that made them sound a little more intelligent than chickens, but I never even heard of anybody eating one. The basic rule for poultry seemed to be, if you can't fry it, you don't want it.

(This pretty much went for eggs, which you could get either sunny-side up or over easy. Both were fried in grease until they turned slightly black at the edges and you needed a sharp object to pierce the yolk. You could get scrambled eggs if you asked or if the cook slipped in cracking the shell, and hard-boiled eggs were a staple at Easter and, deviled, at picnics. But I don't remember seeing a soft-boiled egg served to a healthy person, and I didn't see a poached egg until I was in graduate school. Cheese meant Velveeta and doesn't deserve separate discussion.)

When you could get fresh fish—catfish steaks were best; perch and carp next in that order—from the Missouri or one of its many tributaries, you fried them too. In fact, I don't know from actual observation whether or not the stoves had ovens equipped with broilers.

But fish wasn't really popular. Catholics had to eat a lot of it, so our distaste was understandable. But Protestants didn't care much for it either. Having to clean it was only a minor annoyance. The real trouble was that you couldn't make gravy with it. A meal without a bowl— nothing wimpy and exiguous like a boat—of gravy in the middle of it was nothing but a snack. There were two kinds of gravy, brown and white, from beef and chicken, and both included a lot of flour and pepper. Even my mother could fix pretty good gravy.

Of course, you had to have something to put the gravy on, since it was too thick to drink straight. In an emergency, or in the rare event that you had gravy left over, you could put it on white bread—over the slice if you felt genteel; torn into chunks if you wanted to get right at it without being slowed down by a knife and letting the bread get all soggy. But for the most part, gravy meant potatoes. Potatoes freshly boiled and skinned, a little milk poured in as you pushed down the cross-wired masher.

Mashing potatoes is clearly not genetically transmittable. My father, past seventy, could casually make some of the best mashed potatoes I ever ate. I have rarely tried, and with disastrous results. (I haven't owned a potato masher in more than twenty years, and after one especially notable failure with a borrowed one, I have given up. Besides, who would make the gravy? You can buy it in cans, but there have to be some standards left.) Boiled potatoes were simply mashed potatoes waiting to happen. I seem to remember that we did occasionally eat new potatoes whole, but I associate my first memories of baked potatoes with steak houses in Kansas City. Pasta meant Kraft dinners or the macaroni my mother put into a skillet dish with hamburger and canned tomatoes that she called skullamagoo, from which some varieties of Hamburger Helper are palely descended.

All fresh vegetables aspired to the condition of canned. Most fresh vegetables were seasonal, whether you bought them at the store or grew them yourself or, at peak season, had them forced on you by wild-eyed gardeners forbidden to bring another mess of beans into the house. We didn't equate vegetables with beans quite as often as we did beef with meat, but that was the way to bet. What you did with beans—green beans, of course—was to snap off the ends and break them into half-inch sections (watching Grandma do this was like watching B.B. King take a solo—fast and smooth and casual). Then you put the moist, succulent pieces into a pot full of water with a chunk of bacon or ham, and you boiled them until they turned limp and dark green and safe for human consumption.

All other cooked vegetables were a continuation of beans by other means. Spinach could be revived with vinegar, but stewed tomatoes were hopeless. Stewed okra was, in a friend's unforgettable words, like "something you find in the bottom of an aquarium," and even after she learned that it could be fried, my ex-wife refused not only to cook okra but to have it in the house at all. (We had never heard of gumbo, and not until I ate Acadian food in Nova Scotia did I realize that the British may have done Evangeline and her people a favor by shipping them to the okra belt.) We did a little better with corn on the cob, but "al dente" was a concept as foreign as the words.

Out of season, we depended upon canned goods or the storable kinds of vegetables, roots (the bigger the better, since there was more to them) and, perhaps, in normal families, cabbage. In my family, cabbage was as taboo as human flesh because my mother insistently refused to admit any trace of her German heritage and maintained that cooked cabbage smelled up the house. And so it does, if you cook it for three hours. I don't think I ever saw a squash, winter or summer.

Raw cabbage, in the form of cole slaw, was acceptable. In fact, if it hadn't been for that, we might not have known what a salad was. We did have sweet bell peppers, mostly used to encase stuffing. In season, there were fresh tomatoes and green onions and radishes and even lettuce, but I don't remember that anyone had the idea of putting them all together. Or maybe they were hidden under the off-orange French dressing, apparently named in calculated insult of our former allies, served in tiny bowls in restaurants. When I saw my first chef's salad in the restaurant at Macy's in Kansas City, I could hardly wait for the next day so I could go back and have another. I knew that eating salads wasn't supposed to be manly, but even at seventeen I didn't care. On the other hand, Macy's didn't have anything like Mom's wilted lettuce, so it wasn't pure gain.

My memories of fruit and vegetables are somewhat skewed by the fact that Dad briefly owned a wholesale supply business and used to take me with him to the Kansas City market. I saw and tasted a lot of things not usually available—the only time in my life I could have all the Bing cherries I wanted—and it is hard to separate those experiences from the normal grocery stores. Of course, we had seasonal fruit, some strawberries, a lot of wild blackberries, a few domestic strains like the red raspberries that grew in the alley behind our first home in Boonville and the dewberries left by previous owners of our last. Lots of people had grape arbors behind their houses, but I seem to recall that their grapes were mostly used for jelly. In fact, because of the short seasons, even women without large gardens did a lot of canning because the results were cheaper and tasted better than commercial products. (Besides, a cellar full of mason jars, even more than a locker full of meat, was a sign of family stability because it was right there under your feet.) Apples and pears flourished—there was a commercial apple orchard downriver, reached by an incredibly dusty road, where I picked for a few weeks—and we had plenty of watermelons and canteloupes in season. I remember eating a lot of grapefruit for breakfast and squeezing the juice from the empty halves into a glass or straight down the gullet. That's the only citrus juice I remember. People tell me that they had oranges only in Christmas stockings, and I certainly had them then, but I think I had them more often than that.

We could grow nuts—in fact, large pecan and black walnut trees grew on my father's place—but they were too much trouble to deal with. Nuts were a special Christmas treat—almonds, Brazil nuts (I knew them for years only as "nigger-toes"), English walnuts, and a few pecans, though they had unpleasant associations for my father.

Fruits and nuts were treats rather than desserts. Desserts meant pastries and ice cream. (Or, in the summertime, Jell-o. Actually, only red Jell-o with marshmallows in it was a dessert. Green Jell-o with cole slaw in it was a salad.) Most mothers could bake, and though mine had long since given up the struggle with cakes, she could make pretty good pies. More than fifty years after the event, I vividly remember arriving at my grandparents' house in rural Morgan County incredibly late at night and being brought into a room lighted by a coal oil lamp to eat freshly baked cinnamon rolls. Girls contemporary with me started with brownies and were supposed to work their way up to more advanced forms of baking. You could get store-bought pies and cakes, but that was an admission of something almost shameful—unless, like my mother, who was a proto-existentialist, you were beyond shame.

Ice cream also varied wildly. You could buy it in little cardboard cups, furnished with a flat wooden spoon, and the only difference between the contents and the package was a degree of sweetness. Bulk ice cream had a certain lardlike quality. My family used to peel back the sides of the box and slice the rectangle into slabs, never measured accurately enough to suit everyone, to serve on plates. I don't know that the ice cream was treated with something to retard softening in those days before refrigerators with separate freezers. Anyway, in my family, the knife ensured it never got a chance to soften. (I am happy to say that I have outgrown using a knife to get to the ice cream faster. Microwaving for one minute at half-power does just fine. Repeat if necessary.)

Homemade ice cream was a whole other matter. I don't know whether the difference lay in the ingredients or in the effort we put into turning the crank that turned the paddles inside the metal container, surrounded by salted ice enclosed by a wooden bucket—or maybe in the long wait for the liquid to thicken. But the only difference between the result and what we had been told of heaven was that the ice cream didn't last forever. In fact, grown-ups never used that analogy, which was very shortsighted on the part of the people charged with encouraging vocations. Maybe they had forgotten what ice cream tasted like, in which case being grown-up was even more of a drag than we thought. Anyway, we wouldn't have believed that anything associated with theology could be that pleasant.

Drink was a category separate from food. Liquids at mealtimes weren't pleasant or unpleasant; they were just there to keep the food from getting stuck in your throat. We had stuff to drink at the meal rather than with the meal—milk for the little kids and maybe, depending on family custom, just kids; in the summer, iced tea, often presweetened; coffee for grown-ups. I don't remember that anyone drank water with their meals except in restaurants. I do remember the first time I saw someone order a drink to go with his meal. Dad and Kenny Esser (who owned several liquor stores in town) and I had gone to Kansas City to a basketball game, and when we ordered dinner in an Italian restaurant, Kenny had Chianti with his meal. That was the first time I had ever seen anyone sitting down in a chair to drink wine and the first white man I had ever seen drinking wine at all.

Otherwise, drinks, like Fudgesicles and Popsicles, were recreational rather than nutritional. You were supposed to drink Dr. Pepper at 10, 2, and 4 to break up your day (and to give you a caffeine jolt, though that wasn't mentioned in the ads). Coca-Cola hadn't discovered "You deserve a break today" as a formula, but the idea was certainly there. Lesser brands of soda pop may have had smaller budgets or less inventive agencies, but a lot of them survived: NuGrape, creme soda, cherry soda, strawberry soda, Nehi, Royal Crown Cola, chocolate soda, and dozens of others whose bottles you can find at large flea markets. Many were regional varieties now rolled over by conglomerates.

The same was true of beer. The biggest sellers, then as now, were Budweiser (Busch was not marketed until 1955; Michelob was later; both were designed to pull market shares away from other brands), Schlitz, and Miller. I don't know if Hamm's still exists, and I'm pretty sure that Blatz is gone, and I'm sorry to say that Griesideck is no more (I'm not sure how to spell it but have leaned away from the more obscene possibilities that local pronunciation exploited fully). "Griesideck Brothers Light Lager Beer" sponsored radio broadcasts of the Cardinals games before Gussie Busch bought the team and moved it away from Sportsman's Park. Some of us as big kids professed to believe that the prime qualification for the announcers was to be able to say "Griesideck" two hundred times a game with a straight face. And there were even smaller local breweries. My grandparents owned stock in one in Evansville, and later, when I lived in Madison, Wisconsin, the makers of Centennial Brew knew their customers well enough to send me a Christmas card.

Every beverage cooler—some still using chipped ice, a real treat on a summer's day—was equipped with a device for removing bottle caps, which kids could collect. The misguided would string the caps into circles, insert a mayonnaise jar lid, and call the result an ashtray. Even today, children may be familiar with the kind of opener called a church key, which used to be given away free; then you had to pay for them; now I don't think you can find one to buy. I have one squirreled away in my toolbox in case I have to open a can of paint. But what I don't have, and I bet my children have never seen, is a bottle opener: a contoured strip of metal with a lot of air in the middle, the wider and shorter part of which you put over the bottle cap, the longer and narrower part of which you pushed on for leverage. It was useless for opening cans, which is why the church key supplanted it.

Even milk was different. We used to laugh at city kids who thought that milk grew in bottles, but I doubt that my nieces and nephews who grew up in Boonville with strong ties to the country have ever seen a milk bottle. About ten years ago, at the Canton, Texas, trade days, bigger than the Paris (France) flea market, a companion and I stopped at a stand advertising antiques. She picked up a round cardboard disk a little bigger than a half-dollar (get your father to explain what that is if you've never seen one), with printing on the top and asked what it was. I identified it as a milk bottle cap. Even kids who collected bottle caps never collected these things. And now people make a living from selling them.

Even at the Canton trade days you couldn't find a soda fountain, and it isn't easy to describe one to members of the younger generation, though they may have seen something like it in Archie Comics and "Happy Days" reruns. The big difference from McDonald's, besides the fact that you got to sit down at the counter, was that you could order custom-made drinks that mixed various kinds of flavored syrups. The soda jerk, who didn't get mad when you used that term, had to have a certain amount of skill to mix the various drinks. You could also get sandwiches, but soda fountains were much more important for social than for nutritional purposes—and not just because they didn't have gravy.

In fact, the social mystique of food and drink was separate from the physical stuff. For example, restaurants, which did have gravy, also had a primarily social purpose. In my family, and in a good many others, restaurants meant Sunday dinner, usually at Lawson's Cafe on Morgan Street. The food wasn't all that different from what you ate at home, essentially fried chicken or overcooked beef and vegetables out of cans a lot bigger than those from the A&P, but it looked a little different. The surroundings were not lush—a counter on one side, a few tables in the middle, a few booths along the other wall—but they were at least different. Mom didn't have to cook. The meal had a ceremonial aspect that cowed even the children in my family, and the grown-ups got to see people they knew and let other grown-ups see them functioning in public as a family—not, despite nostalgic views of the nuclear family in the postwar period, all that common even in a small town.

Church suppers were special occasions not only because they didn't happen very often but because you got to go through a line and choose from different kinds of food. (There wasn't, to my knowledge, a cafeteria within a hundred miles.) Actually, the dishes weren't all that different from those we ate at home or from each other except that the casseroles were more highly colored and there seemed to be a lot more marshmallows on top of the sweet potatoes and red Jell-o. But here, as elsewhere, quantity rather than variety was important. And you got to see a lot of different people.

In my family, meals at home were not a social occasion. I don't re- member that we ever had anyone over to dinner. Guests and kids' friends sat at our table often enough—the table in the big kitchen, that is—but the dining room table was useful mostly to keep the larger males from banging their heads on the light fixture. It was only used at Thanksgiving and Christmas, when Grandpa and Grandma Murray would come across the back yard and Uncle Bob and Aunt Goldie would drive up from Otterville and everyone would eat—turkey, ham, mashed potatoes and dressing and gravy and sweet potatoes and several kinds of vegetables and canned jellied cranberries and stuffed celery and two or three kinds of pie—until they could barely stagger away from the table. You knew that you were getting to be a man when you could eat with them fork to fork; they acknowledged your prowess by teasing you about it. Then the women would retire to the kitchen to deal with the dishes, and the men would walk out to the pasture, if weather permitted, and lean on the fence and look over the land and whatever livestock happened to be visible. When the weather didn't permit, the men sat in the living room and told stories (more lethargically than usual) because there was no television. That was pretty Norman Rock-wellish. We even had a grace before the meal—my grandfather kept his views to himself—but not at the end.

On normal days, mealtime at my house looked as if somebody had turned over a rock. Except when my mother got to feeling guilty and insisted on fixing oatmeal on winter mornings, kids were responsible for getting their own breakfast—not hard, since we had boxed cereal, though nothing like the variety available now. (When my children were little, we had more different brands on our shelves than any grocery store anywhere in the late forties.) Dinner, the noon meal, was supposed to be the big meal of the day, but unless we had a cook, my parents' work and our school undercut that. All or maybe most of the family would show up for supper, depending on our schedules or Dad's work, and since he bought and sold things freelance, the only thing you could predict about his schedule was that you couldn't anticipate it.

Anyway, eating was not exactly a communal experience at our house. All of us liked to eat and most of us liked to talk, but not at the same time. We ate as if the food might run out, like middle distance runners who have learned to sprint the whole way, and since ambidexterity runs in the male line, we didn't have to waste time putting down our knives and shifting our forks to the other hand. In fact, the food never did run out: we grew lots of potatoes, the Jersey cow gave enough milk to support even my gallon-a-day habit (Mom got tired of passing the milk and bought me a tin cup that held a quart), and the refrigerator was always full. Sometimes with surprising stuff. I came home one night, only a little the worse for drink, and opened the door to find a calf's head staring back at me. My mother once encountered the frozen carcass of a fox. This was my brother's zoology project, though, not a culinary experiment.

When I go back to Boonville now, food seems a lot more like that found everywhere else than it used to. Restaurants have ceased to be social centers, except for men taking a break from work to drink coffee or have a late breakfast or lunch. During my visits, we eat out on weekdays, when women as well as men have been at work. Anyway, Lawson's has disappeared, Holt's Cafe, which doubled as the Greyhound bus station, has long since closed, and Pete Jr. moved Pete's Cafe from Highway 40 on Main Street to a spot ten miles east on Interstate 70, where it went belly up some years ago. Some nonfranchise restaurants still dot downtown Boonville, but the real action is near the bend where Highway 40 turns west—a Dairy Queen, which opened in 1949 or 1950 as a walk-up and is now much expanded; Hardee's; the Colonel; A&W—and at the three interchanges with I-70. Big John's, a trolley-shaped greasy spoon diner a few blocks west, is a living fossil. One restaurant, open only on weekends, serves old-style food, the meat better than the bread, the bread better than the vegetables, but otherwise you would have to drive to Columbia, twenty-odd miles east, to find more exotic or lovingly prepared food—to dine rather than eat.

Home-cooked food is a little different too. Boonville now has two supermarkets, neither belonging to a national chain, and no grocery stores named for their owners. They stock more things, most of which taste better and almost all of which are more convenient, than the stores of forty years ago. I don't know if they have bean sprouts because it never occurs to me to look, but they have greater variety in the produce section.

People still grow their own vegetables, and you can buy early corn from some of the farmers. My brother can still buy into a beef carcass if he wants to—he has good German in-laws in the business. His refrigerator is jammed, or was until his son and last daughter moved out. My sister, who remodeled the kitchen at the Place but left room for a big table, commutes to work a little farther than she used to, and you can only count on finding cereal, milk, and ice cream in her pantry and refrigerator. Judging from my yearly visits, it is a rare occasion for either family to sit down together even before the kids went away to college and beyond. The only time our extended family gets together is on holidays or when I turn up, and even then people charge in and out on various errands. We eat a lot of beef that my sister-in-law fixes. My sister and her daughter bake some pies. There's still a big bowl of mashed potatoes but an even bigger bowl of salad because my baking niece is also very health-conscious. It's not at all clear whether a third generation of our family will live in that house. Everybody is too busy and grown-up to tend even an electric ice cream freezer. Anyway, the barn is empty, so we wouldn't have the homegrown cream to put in it.

On the other hand, I don't have to get up at six o'clock on a raw morning and milk that g.d. cow.

Work and Play

Late in the afternoon on a hot August day in 1957. I had come home after a summer of working on my master's thesis before leaving to study for a doctorate. The thick walls of the house and the high ceiling of the living room shut out most of the heat, and I sat in an easy chair, a notepad on one arm, a bourbon and water over ice on the other, a book in my lap.

My father entered the front door and came through the hall into the living room. He was hot. He may have remembered his father and the set of Bulwer-Lytton novels. He was moving, and I was sitting down. He slowed, but didn't stop, and said, "When you going to get off your ass and do some work?"

Nearly twenty-three, I was used to carrying on a conversation with a moving target. "I am working, Dad. This is what I do when I work."

"Bullshit!" And he disappeared through the door to the dining room on his way to the kitchen.

Ten years later, a not-so-young assistant professor trying to publish enough to make a name for myself, I stopped at the door of the department's senior professor and most distinguished scholar to say hello. With the kind of diffidence that comes from complete confidence, he said, "I hope you won't think I'm impertinent, but some of us are concerned that you are working so hard that you will injure your health."

I thanked him for his concern, assured him that I felt fine, and added,

"I can't wait to tell my father that, but I'm not going to tell him over the phone. I want to see his face." With Dad, you had to be able to read faint signs. He almost never laughed, and he rarely smiled. But when I told him the story, his lip twitched just a little. Perhaps he didn't remember what Grandpa Murray said on hearing him praised for being hard-working: "Well, it's no wonder. He got enough rest when he was young."

More than ten years later, several days into my annual visit, Dad and I were looking out over his lawn. I noticed that the large lilac bush by the fence between lawn and pasture was full of volunteer maple trees, and I went over and pulled up some of the smaller ones. Soon I had a trimming saw and tree-trimming tool and had moved out of the lilac bush to take care of the fencerow. Dad finally got his electric saw and took care of the thickest trunks. After a while, we were dusty, scratched a little here and there, and wet through with sweat. But the lilac bush and fence were a lot cleaner. Still, the pasture side of the fence was littered with debris from our work, and I suggested that we get the tractor and trailer, load up the trash, and take it down to the hollow to retard erosion.

"No," Dad said, "let's leave it for a while." A pause. Then, almost plaintively, "You worked me too hard."

I raised my eyes to heaven and said, only part mockingly, "Thank you, God!" I had become an adult.

The real difference between grown-ups and kids was that grown-ups worked. And they did it when no one was watching or telling them what to do next, and apparently they did stuff with no concrete end in view, at least that kids could see.

Kids didn't work; they did chores. Chores were sometimes onerous, like cutting grass or weeding the garden or washing the dishes. (In some families, this might have been considered girls' work, but I had to wait ten years for a sister, my brother five, and by the time she got big enough to trust with dishes, I had left for college. So I washed a lot of dishes.)

Sometimes the chores were hard work, like pushing a hand cultivator through two acres of garden. Chopping wood was hard, but it didn't have to be done in full sunlight, and besides, being trusted with an ax was heady stuff, at least at first. Sometimes chores were downright disgusting, like dredging stale cow piss from the clogged drainage trough of the barn with a bucket. It was cheaper and easier to order a kid to do it than to bring out a plumber to clear the drain or dig it up and repair it.

Sometimes chores were punitive. When my friends and I decided that we were grown-up enough to experiment with alcohol and carried on the experiment too enthusiastically, Dad never wasted his breath in sorrow or anger about my coming in late and drunk. In fact, he never mentioned the fact—even at six o'clock in the morning, when he would wake me up and send me out to cut fencerow with a two-handed brush-cutter. Hitting a wire fence with one of those certainly focused my attention even if it didn't make me mend my ways. It did make him feel that he had taken appropriate action, and it allowed me to pay, in full, my debt to respectability. And after a while it turned cold sweat into hot sweat.

By this time, it had began to occur to me, dimly, that chores had more than one meaning. I could see that the dishes got washed, which meant that we could eat off them again; the garden kept relatively free of weeds, which meant that we had fresh vegetables to eat; and the trash carried out of sight down to the ravine ("holler" in local dialect), which slowed down the process of erosion. And I learned the hard way from Dad that all this could have a therapeutic as well as a moral value.

But it didn't seem as interesting as play. For one thing, most chores were solitary. For another, they didn't earn you any peer approval. No matter how neatly you cut the grass, for example, you did it by yourself, and while you could get some satisfaction from completing a pattern in cutting the lawn, this was clearly an act of desperation, and you wouldn't get a rush if you cut grass better than any kid on the block.

Play seemed superior not because it caused less mental or physical stress—it sometimes caused more—but because it offered immediate gratification. Building a dam down at the creek involved as much work as most chores, but you got to see the water back up and you knew that you didn't have to do it again if you didn't want to. More physical kinds of play rehearsed skills—stealth, alertness, speed—you would need as a successful predator or athlete, but the real point was the adrenaline rush you got from competition.

Hide-and-go-seek seemed the best game for a long time because it was the purest. You had to calculate hairline fractions of relative speed, distance, and the guard's attention before you burst from hiding toward the base. War games, including cowboys and Indians, were more exciting because you were stalker and prey at the same time and quickness of hand and eye were more important. (Indians weren't very popular. We preserved stereotyped Japanese and Nazis a little beyond the end of the Second World War but had gotten too old by the time Russians became popular foes, and when North Koreans and Chinese Communists had come to our attention, we were almost old enough for real guns.) Besides, movies and boys' books provided outlines of scripts to follow, and even if you played the bad guy, you participated in a satisfying ritual in which everyone knew the right moves. Anyway, the rules were open to interpretation, and some revisionist historians probably got a start debating thesis and antithesis of "I shot you first" and "No, you didn't."

Neighborhood games provided a kind of test, but, perhaps because they involved kids of different ages and even sexes and occurred in clearly defined territory—my house, your yard—and offered clear lines of honorable retreat, they were essentially pacific. Playground games, at least the really good ones that the nuns always dispersed, hinted at a nature red in tooth and claw. You had to be quick, evasive, and strong to play pum-pum-poloway, in which the kid who was "it" tried to tag—sometimes bulldog—those running across his space. You had to be strong to play red rover, in which, one at a time, kids tried to burst through a chain of arms linked against them, seeking, if cunning, the weakest pair, or if showing bravado, the strongest.

Everybody soon knew which was which. We didn't have to have experience with chickens to know about pecking orders, especially when any dispute, physical or metaphysical, could be satisfactorily settled by a punch in the nose. And despite our good Catholic upbringing, it seemed obvious that it was better to be the puncher than the punched and that a strong enough deterrent can be very effective. The nuns were like the United Nations—not always there and always too late to prevent initial strikes. (Maybe someone should study the relationship between politicians' experience of playground bullies and foreign policy, though I doubt that they would be willing to talk about it.) Parents were ambivalent: they didn't want you to fight, but they didn't want you to lose. In fact, some boys never seemed to have to fight, perhaps because they were larger or less competitive or loud-mouthed—had, in short, better social survival skills. Nobody really got hurt, because a playground fight was a lot like a brawl in major league baseball—lots of pushing and shoving and lying on top of people, but no kneeing or gouging or dangerous weapons. They were more like battles between males of sensible species where a clear show of superiority ends the fight. It was very gratifying to get to the point where one could show it.

The energy devoted to these kinds of contests began, by the time we were twelve or thirteen, to be channeled into more formally competitive sports. This meant team sports, mainly baseball, which was so important that it deserves a separate chapter, but we also began to play basketball and football in driveways and vacant lots. Individual sports were more like hobbies. Some kids who hung out at the golf course to caddy became notable golfers. (Nobody played tennis except the cadets at Kemper Military School, and they represented whole other regions, classes, and ways of life.) A few white kids went to the swimming pool every day—I certainly did—and though that was not really a competitive sport as we understood the term, you had to pass an endurance test to be allowed in the deep end. Swimming lessons were available, but for some reason I thought them undignified, and I doggedly set about teaching myself until I became the third best swimmer in the Catholic grade school. I don't remember that there was a fourth, but I got a lot of gross motor exercise and a world-class suntan.

About this time we seemed to be expected to develop skills useful to society. Some kids from the country—not Catholic school boys, for reasons I never understood—began to turn up in Future Farmers of America jackets and 4-H Club patches, showing cattle at fairs and exhibiting canned goods and sewing projects at local fairs. Girl Scouts made fewer public displays of their talents, but they too seemed to be getting ready for grown-up life. By contrast, Boy Scouts seemed kind of pointless. Even if you could learn to name and even tie all those knots (I never did), what good would they do you? The same thing seemed true of most of the merit badge activities: they were arcane or pointless. Or, worse, they overlapped school subjects. At that time, I didn't know that Baden-Powell had founded the Scouts in the wake of the Boer War to prepare city boys to become better soldiers. But we did know that scouts were vaguely goody-goody, and in my troop we tried to form a "skunk patrol" of those who never got past Tenderfoot. Our scoutmaster blocked this, and many of us dropped out. We discovered that we could do the same things—cut down trees, build fires, camp out—all by ourselves, free of adult supervision, and be just as uncomfortable as if we were amassing merit toward a higher state of being. Merit badges resembled the indulgences we learned about in the catechism, though more concrete and of less spiritual and very little practical value, birdhouses not being high on our list of priorities.

Anyway, I soon got enough of the open spaces. When I was about twelve or thirteen, my family moved to the Place. Within a year or so, my mother's parents moved in with us while Grandpa converted the carriage shed into a two-bedroom house. Perhaps in any case I would have spent more time with adults, but because I was big enough to do some work and because I had left my former neighborhood friends all the way across town and couldn't find new ones my age, I spent a lot more time with my family.

Some of it was spent in play. My father used to play cards with me, which was very instructive since he had run the poker game in the basement of his pool hall and was good enough on his own that, home from a trip to Las Vegas in his mid-seventies and asked how he did, he replied, "Made expenses." But he didn't always make expenses, and I was also becoming aware that his gambling, like his periodic drinking, contained an element of self-punishment. Grandpa Murray seemed different because he seemed to enjoy the moment rather than the result. He played checkers with me, or at me. He could see five moves further ahead than I. Neither Dad nor Grandpa were hypocritical or shortsighted enough to let me win in order to boost my self-esteem. The difference was that Dad would scoop up a trick poker-faced and Grandpa would chortle in delight as he jumped three of my men and wound up in king's row.

Dad made play seem like work. And work was deadly serious. When I got old enough to tease him—about age 35—I told him that his motto ought to be, "If it feels good, you must be doing it wrong." When concentrating on a physical or mechanical job, he would stick his tongue between his teeth at one edge of his mouth and frown in concentration. My major contribution to repair jobs was holding the flashlight while mysterious stuff went on in the bowels of whatever it was. Every job was a test with no make-up. The worst beating I ever got—bad enough that it was the last—was because, even though I had not been told to, I had not fed the pigs on my own initiative. (At least that was the only reason I was ever given. Having since been a parent myself, I wonder if something else might not have been going on.)

Looking back, I can see that Dad was more intense than anything else. It was always surprising to find that he could play. For Christmas (of 1941, I think) he got me a full electric train set, the better for being used because the tracks were already mounted on big boards, which he set up in the basement of the duplex on Fourth Street and played with for hours to wind down after a run on the Katy. Later he would sometimes stop by the basketball goal he had installed under the walnut trees, call for the ball, and throw up, while moving, the kind of two-handed underhand shot popular in his high school days. I only remember his playing catch with me once, when he demonstrated how to throw a curveball. For several days afterward he moved his right arm carefully, and as with various other situations, I sympathize more now than I did then. But the only time he really surprised me was at his wholesale fruit and vegetable business. We were unloading a truckload of watermelons, and Dad promised that if one got broken, we could take it home. We had almost finished, with no damage, and I was starting to worry. Dad looked over the few remaining, hefted the most promising knee-high, looked at me, grinned slightly, lowered the melon to shin level, and dropped it. It may not have been the best-tasting melon I ever had, but it was the most satisfying.

Grandpa Murray, on the other hand, never seemed to strain, and he made work seem like play. Throughout any task, and I am still convinced that he could handle anything short of brain surgery, he was either whistling, always the same tune that I never heard anywhere else (to save my kids the trouble, the tune I whistle while thinking of something else is Tommy Ladnier's "Mojo Strut," or as close as I can get to it) or swearing, either at the materials or at his helper. But he let me try to hammer nails, taught me how to pull and straighten the ones I had bent, and showed me a better technique with the hammer. He and I built a chute for loading cattle, which still stands under the catalpa tree in the empty barnyard. It should. It has about forty pounds of nails in it, and it will rust before it collapses. A lot of adrenaline went into it too: "Goddamn it, Bobby, that nail's not long enough! You need at least a tenpenny to keep the son-of-a-bitch from working loose! No, goddamn it, a sixteen penny will split that board like a bull stepping on a dry shingle! Hell, you don't have to beat it to death! You're as bad as your Dad! You'd have to use dynamite to get it out now!" I haven't got it right, but that's as close as I can get.

For Grandpa, a job seemed to be a game that you could keep playing until you got it right, and if you got it wrong, it didn't matter because he could make it come out. For someone as irascible as he was on the surface, he could be surprisingly patient, and he could work with delicate mechanical problems that his more physical son-in-law and grandson would botch by applying the theory, "Don't force it; get a bigger hammer," or abandon in frustration.

What Grandpa really liked to do, though, was talk, and it didn't seem to make much difference what he talked about. Like any good performer, he preferred first-rate accompaniment, but he could solo as long as he wanted. He had definite opinions on everything, especially politics, and especially the shortcomings if not downright iniquities of the Democratic party. He also had definite opinions on religion, but in deference to the way I was being raised, he was uncharacteristically silent about them with me. He was a good explainer once I learned to filter out his opinions. He was particularly good at tall tales of which he was never the butt. Sometimes my father was the protagonist, which delighted us, and even my father would smile just a little as the story of his being abandoned in the New Mexico mountains grew into the saga of the Year of the Great Holler that Dad supposedly gave to call for help.

But even better than tall tales, Grandpa liked arguing, preferably, since he was very well informed, about points of fact. I only caught him once. He had said that the Phoenicians came from the west end of the Mediterranean, and I insisted that they came from the east end and, to his surprise, proved it with a book taken from his shelf. He countered by pointing out that the Phoenicians had established colonies at the west end and sputtered a little when I countered that colonizing wasn't "coming from." I think he was pleased that I showed signs of becoming a verbal sparring partner. (Mom liked to argue too, but she was never wrong or at least never got pinned down to admitting it.)

Grandpa never overtly seemed to be teaching me anything, and I don't remember his ever talking to me as adult to child. But I learned a lot because he took me places where adult things were going on. The most instructive trip, though none were boring, was to the state capital, Jefferson City. Grandpa had given up any plans to run for office by the time he moved to Boonville, but he did become county chairman of the Republican party. When he learned that our state representative, Jake Meyer, had promised to vote against local interests on a trucking bill, he had to go to Jefferson City to minimize the damage. He took me with him, and on the way he told me that he wasn't even going to try to get Jake to reverse his vote because that would make him look bad for breaking a promise. Instead, he was going to try to convince Jake to take a walk when the house voted on the bill. We went to Jake's hotel room, and when Jake offered him whiskey and raised one eye-brow toward me, Grandpa said, "He's my grandson, isn't he," and a third shot was poured. I didn't care much for the taste of whiskey, but I was very proud of the recognition. And in listening to them talk, I learned more about the political process than in all my civics lessons combined.

With the physical energy of the Davis side and the verbal energy of the Murray side, it wasn't surprising that the kids played with a lot of verbal and physical energy. In my family, dishwashing was a competi-tive sport without any rules but a lot of debating over who had done which last time with what success. We had the closest thing to full con-tact croquet that I have ever seen. The front yard, with five or six large trees and a lot of exposed roots, was bounded by a state highway, a sunken driveway, a wire fence, and the house shielded by low-growing evergreens. The real object was to hit the other person's ball as far as you could—out-of-bounds rules were specifically excluded—and pro-voke a shriek of indignation. My baby sister couldn't hit as hard, but she was at no disadvantage because she was at least as loud as the rest of us and had a more penetrating voice.

In fact, making her yell enough to get the attention of adults without drawing their wrath was almost a sanctioned sport. Once my brother lured her into playing cowboys and Indians by letting her be the cow-boy. Then he tied her to the clothesline post, laid a circular fire, and lit it. She knew that this was what Indians did to cowboys, so she stood mute. To achieve the desired end, he told her that the post was full of termites and that the fire would cause them to come out and eat her. That produced a howl strong enough to bring Mom from the other end of the house to save her daughter from the fire and probably to heat up her son's hind end.

Except for the nightly dishwashing contests, we didn't work together much. My brother did get told off to help me clean the barn, and in order to shorten the job of cleaning the barn trough, I carried the five-gallon bucket full of rancid cow piss to the board pasture fence, climbed it, and waited for him to hand it over to me. Several buckets into the job, one caught on the top board and dumped the load over my lower half. My brother was across the barnyard, over the next fence, and halfway to the house and adult protection before the bucket hit the ground. He said later that it was an accident, and if I find out different tomorrow, forty years later, I'll still kill him.

We didn't get paid directly for even the most onerous of these chores, but for years, in my family and most others, we received an allowance to help us learn to manage money, an insidious way of chaining us to the cash economy. The first thing I learned was that if you blow the whole allowance at the dime store, you don't have any more. If not the second thing, a fairly early thing was that your desires expand past your income. That means that you have to get more money.

There weren't a lot of ways for kids to earn money. There were two kinds of newspaper routes. Carrying the Kansas City *Times* and *Star* was more lucrative than carrying the Boonville *Daily News*, but it was a major commitment because it involved thirteen deliveries a week, very early every morning and evening six days a week, plus collecting for papers. Carrying the *Daily News* took five evenings a week, collecting done by the circulation manager rather than the boys, but it paid about $3.60 a week depending upon the number of papers you delivered. Both types of routes were handed down like season tickets in a successful football program, which may have accounted for the fact that no Catholic school kids carried the *Star*.

Looking at that schedule, I learned that I did not want money that badly. But since even at the *Daily* you could get fired for not showing up and docked ten cents for every complaint about an undelivered paper, I guess we learned responsibility. Since my route wound up and down several steep hills, I learned to pump my Monkey Ward bike hard enough to steer with one hand and throw papers with the other, with the result that my calves grew bigger than my thighs and stayed that way for an alarmingly long time. And I learned that you could take a kind of stubborn pride in completing a trivial job under really lousy conditions without expecting any recognition. On my most miserable day as a paperboy there was a cold, soaking winter rain. The front fender of my bicycle, twisted beyond repair, had been removed, and I was getting wet from both top and bottom. By the time I reached my house, some twenty papers and about a mile round-trip from the end of the route, I was wet through a heavy coat to the skin and too uncomfortable to go on. After I stripped, dried, and dressed, I found another coat and finished the route, pleased with myself because I was doing what I was supposed to do without being told. I had skipped the Training School Dairy, a three-block round-trip for a single paper. Duty was duty, but I was willing to give up the lousy ten cents.

Paper boys worked for adults, but they did not work with adults, and carrying papers was clearly a kid's job. Even so, poor kids held on to *Star* routes until they could get jobs alongside their parents at the shoe factory. But middle-class kids, tired of low pay and low status and lousy working conditions, tended to drop out at fourteen or earlier. There weren't a lot of other ways to earn money, and most of them were extensions of chores: cutting grass, cleaning things up and putting them away (stock boy), or fixing drinks and washing dishes (soda jerk). These paid a little better, or at least gave you more hours, and they were indoors—and, though we wouldn't have put it that way, gave us some standing on the lowest rung of the adult world.

That, more than the money, seems to me now the real reason that we wanted jobs. Some of my friends worked not because they really needed the money but because their fathers thought that it would be good for them. But basically you worked because that is what real people did.

It was satisfying to be able to meet the expectation that you would be able to earn money to pay incidental expenses and to save something for a college education. We also began to realize that working expanded your social life, most obviously for the guys who worked at Foster's soda fountain and got to see everybody who came in, increasingly including girls.

And we became dimly aware that some jobs were more interesting than others. Through vague and complicated ties of influence, I got somewhere around my junior year in high school a real indoor job at the recently opened Dairy Queen. It paid fifty cents an hour—good money in those days—and enough hours promised in the summer and even in the school year ahead to be really useful, with enough flexibility to accommodate my athletic and social career. The working conditions were close to ideal because the customers couldn't get inside to make a mess we'd have to wipe up and because my coworker was a sensible, efficient, and good-natured classmate whose talents later took him to a management job with a big company in St. Louis. All we had to do was keep the place clean, including the large and somewhat complicated machine, be respectful to people who needed respect, and shove frozen custard through the little hatches at the front of the building.

Since I had been dealing with grown-ups all my life, since I had experience with disassembling, cleaning, and reassembling an old-fashioned cream separator, and since I had a number of peers who could be very unpleasant, I soon realized that I could handle anything the job required. Highway 40 passed right in front of us, and we could even get glimpses of a larger, more interesting, and somewhat scarier world. One day a gleaming convertible—a Packard, I think—nosed up to the stand and a sharply dressed man in his late twenties got out. In a chatty mood after a long stretch on the road, he told us that he was a musician and invited us to look over his car, leather seats and all.

The seats, he mentioned casually, posed a real hazard to girls wearing bathing suits who sat on them in the hot sun. I don't know how my companion felt, but I couldn't decide what I envied most, the car or the casual way he talked about all those women.

This kind of stimulation didn't come along every day, but the Dairy Queen offered enough variety to keep me interested. Then I heard that there was an opening for an all-round apprentice at the Cooper County *Record*, a shabby and would-be maverick newspaper. It paid twenty cents an hour to start. I may have thought about it a little and may even have consulted my parents, but I didn't hesitate long because I was certain that I wanted to be a newspaper reporter and live a glamorous life in a big city with a cigarette hanging from the side of my mouth as I banged out an exclusive story on my typewriter.

The *Record* wasn't nearly that glamorous. In fact, the owner, publisher, and editor, E. J. Melton, would hand-feed the big, noisy flatbed press and then the folding machine himself, stripped to his undershirt. There was a receptionist-secretary-bookkeeper and a linotype operator. My job was to do everything that the other three people didn't do, from sweeping the sidewalk in front to writing minor news stories to casting cuts and feeding the job press in the back room to carrying trash out the back.

The only obvious skill I retain from that job is the ability to read upside down, and contemporary printers don't need that. If you wanted to burn yourself in a contemporary cold-type shop, you would have to bring matches with you. The kind of equipment we used can be found only in the Smithsonian or in the more chi-chi antique shops. Some people still write and read the same kind of stories in smalltown weeklies across the country, the kind I buy while passing through in fits of nostalgia.

I learned a lot from Old Man Melton, including not to try to be too fancy with words and not to act superior to the people and situations you write about. But he was less important to me because of what he did than because of what he was. What impressed me most was that he was a writer. He had published a history of Cooper County and a novel, *Towboat Pilot*, an older juvenile that had a modest success a couple of years before I went to work for him. (He had also written another novel, a roman à clef based on people and events in Boonville, which he was never able to publish. This was a good way of learning about the writer's life.) As a newspaperman of long experience, he had contacts with a world larger than and very different from Boonville. He was notorious for saying what he thought and for thinking different things from everyone else. The idea that you could make a living directly from reading and writing and generally making a nuisance of yourself appealed to me a good deal. I admired my grandfather, but he maintained his amateur standing in these respects.

However, this was still a kid's job, though a big kid's job that taught a variety of skills and, as they now say, looked good on the résumé. The really serious jobs for young men involved hard physical labor— pipeline and highway work—but they seemed to be reserved for football players, and the Catholic high school was too small and too poor to field a team. Many town kids got jobs bucking bales in the hay fields, and a few went west and followed the wheat harvest north for the summer. These jobs tested the most obvious kinds of manhood—strength, endurance, guts.

I didn't get a job like this until I came home after my first year of college. There didn't seem to be any jobs, so Dad put me to work painting the woodwork on the house. I had got part way down the front door when he came home and announced that he had found me a job at the Missouri Farmers' Association elevator over by the Katy tracks. As I went in to clean up, I heard him say, "God damn! Now I'll have to do it myself." But a job clearly outranked a mere chore.

The MFA job fully convinced me that I wanted to be a member

of the middle class, indeed, of the professional class. Part of the job was unloading boxcars full of sacks. Fertilizer sacks weighed only sixty pounds, but they burned the skin on contact. Feed sacks weighed a hundred pounds and had to be stacked ten high. For the first week on the job, I couldn't do that. The loud redneck with the stomach hanging over his belt could. What the hell, he outweighed my 160 pounds by almost half. But so could the small, quiet, elderly man with the blue workshirt buttoned at the cuffs, the bib overalls, and the billed denim cap. I had no choice but to learn, and with his example and advice, I did. By the end of the summer I was six inches wider at the shoulder, but I still weighed 160 pounds. None of it was water retention.

Another job was preparing boxcars to receive wheat from the elevator. Essentially, what you did was close out most of the air. Three wooden forms of double boards weighing about thirty pounds each had to be boosted up and dragged into the car and nailed one above the other over each door. A little room was left at the top, not so you could get out but so the wheat could be funneled in. This was in late June and early July in mid-Missouri, when the temperature in the shade is in the 90s and the humidity as close to 100 percent as it can get with the sky cloudless. One day I finished nailing, tossed the hammer out the narrow gap at the top, and sat down to catch my breath and gather the energy to clamber out. Suddenly it occurred to me—I was not a quick thinker—"There has got to be an easier way!" And I began to consider what kind of jobs would allow me to sit at a desk in an air-conditioned office.

Still, I lasted the summer, both physically and socially. Looking back, I can see that all of us had an odd status in these temporary jobs. Structurally, we were part-time and dispensable gofers, items in a long series of high school and even just kids holding dead-end jobs where no one ever learned anything about the way that businesses were run or anything else that would be useful except for building character. But we weren't just temporary; we were mobile, and some of us were clearly upwardly mobile.

That put us in an odd relationship to adults whose skills and responsibilities were extensions of chores and who would never have any more interesting or lucrative work. The surprising thing to me was—and is— that while they might tease us and send us on rookie errands, they never seemed to resent us. The worst I ever encountered in a temporary job was indifference or a kind of defensive bravado, and several men were surprisingly supportive. Paul Fox, the linotype operator at the Cooper County *Record*, told me that if I decided not to do something more challenging and important, he would help me get into the school where he had been trained. The manager of the Missouri Farmers' Association tried to interest me in an assistant manager's job when I got a little older than seventeen, and the men with whom I loaded and unloaded hundred-pound sacks of feed never tried to exclude me even though they knew that at the end of the summer I would go back to college and on into the white-collar world. A couple of years later, when I worked Saturdays as a janitor, the custodian remarked with obvious pleasure that I wouldn't have to do this kind of work all my life.

While I was pleased that they thought me competent, because I was often nervous that I wouldn't be, I'm not sure why they had this attitude. It may have been the result of the Depression generation's satisfaction that they were making it possible for their successors to live otherwise. (This almost avuncular interest in the younger generation was the positive side of the attitude that allowed any grown-up to yell at any kid. There was a sense of continuity that I'm not sure we have now.) Or it may have been because I never felt superior to the people, who knew more about what was going on here than I did, or to the job. The custodian was surprised that he didn't have to tell this particular college kid to mop behind the doors. Clearly he never had dealings with my father.

Dad wasn't always as grim as he might sound or as serious as he may have felt he had to be to set the right example. In fact, I began to suspect that he regarded life not just as a test but a series of contests. He had done a lot of things, and it was always a dilemma what to put down in the blanks after "father's occupation." "Trader" seemed to connote the South Seas. "Dealer" was OK until the current connotation got locked in. What he actually did, or did best, was buy and sell things: cars, cattle, farm machinery, almost anything that wasn't nailed down and some things that were. He would come home from a successful deal looking different from usual—in fact, a lot like Grandpa after he had triple-jumped.

The two men got on so well that I have never really understood in-law jokes. Dad didn't talk for recreation, but he admired good talk. And he admired a good trader even more. Once I stood across the back yard from the two as they pointed out to a customer the virtues of Grandpa's 1940 Ford coupe, which they were trying to sell him. It looked like a kung fu movie with the sound turned off, though the ritualized gestures were slower. You didn't need subtitles to follow a plot in which the opponent had as little chance as Bruce Lee's.

In fact, though I think of my father as solitary, he had a number of trading partners over the years. Once it was a mentor, like Old Man Darby, whose own son was rather feckless, with whom he bought farm property. Once it was a younger man, like Sam Jewett, blond, voluble, and open in contrast to Dad's laconic and rather Heathcliffian darkness. Once it was Ham Horst, who resembled Dad in many ways but had connections in the nearby town of Pilot Grove that Dad could use. Actually, I don't think he needed any of these partners, except maybe the first. He was a good enough hunter to flush and bag his own game.

What he really needed, I suspect, was someone to watch the cunning and technique with which he did it. Unlike the stereotypical used car salesman, who surrounds his prey and stuns it with noise, Dad sometimes acted as if he didn't care whether he sold or bought the item or not. Confronted by an anxious seller, he would pull out his billfold and start counting out $20, $50, and $100 bills, saying, "Tell you what I'm going to do." Pause. "I'll give you a thousand dollars cash for it right *now*." With a different kind of opponent, stuck at an impasse between asking and selling price after a long bargaining session, he would say, "Tell you what." Pause. "I'll flip you for the difference." This let the other party know that this deal was a game, not life and death, and it either unstuck the bargaining or created a different kind of excitement. He was not only dealing, he was playing dealer.

If he didn't have a better audience, he would sometimes play to me when I got older. Like the other dealers at the Kansas City Auto Auction, he prided himself on being a quick judge of cars and so silent and unobtrusive a bidder that only the auctioneer's spotter could see him. Once, when I was grown and visiting with my wife, he insisted, with his mock casual, "come on and go with me" that I accompany him to a farm auction. He glanced at a tractor, and during the course of the auction gave three different answers about its probable worth to people who came up to benefit from his expertise and cunning. When it went under the hammer, I stood beside him as he remained silent. As we left, I wondered who had bought the tractor. With great and understated satisfaction, he said "I did" and named a price lower than any he had quoted. Then I realized that he had not only been showing off but having fun. And I was surprised and touched that he needed me to see this and to admire his skill.

My father taught me almost everything about work—finally, even, that it could be more fun than nominal play—except how to do what he did, and that was because, knowing I was incompetent, I didn't even try to learn. In fact, the fathers of my contemporaries did not pass on this kind of knowledge. Of the boys I can trace from my crowd, only one, a farmer, does anything like what his father did. Or where he did it. The fathers weren't holding out on us; they wanted us to live different lives and finally, I think, my father was pleased that I did. If he never understood what I do when I work, he was glad to have a son clever enough to get away with doing whatever it was and energetic enough to do a lot of it. If it was a bluff, it was a bluff a good card-player could respect.

Because he went to bed about 9:00 P.M., I never managed to get up in the morning before he did. But I get up a lot earlier and more voluntarily than I used to, I go to work a lot more willingly, and I enjoy doing it a lot more than I do most forms of play. He didn't necessarily want me to go out and clear that last fencerow, but I suspect that despite his exhaustion he was pleased that I hadn't forgotten how to do a job that wasn't mine without having to be told and how to insist on carrying it through to the end.

Later I told the story to his oldest surviving friend and added, "Working for Dad makes every job I've had since look easy." Dad snorted, and I don't know whether or not he believed me. He should have. And it should have pleased him.

Scoring and Playing

Miles away from Boonville, years later. My students, when told that D. H. Lawrence had probably been impotent for several years when he wrote *Lady Chatterley's Lover*, think it presumptuous for a man with that kind of handicap to write about sex and perhaps even about love. Trying, as patiently as I could manage, to explain memory and imagination to people with no concept of either, I speculated that although I had not played baseball in thirty-five years, I could probably write about it much more convincingly than I could have at eighteen. When the most indignant student countered that of course it was easy to reproduce a box score, I knew how Socrates must have felt when someone posed a more than usually fat and stupid objection, because a box score gives as little experience of the game as a sex manual does of making love.

I have nothing against sex manuals and box scores, because even when you can't actually do something, you can remember it, anticipate it, study your moves, plan more moves. Sex manuals are a lot more helpful than they used to be, but the box scores now carried in the daily papers are much less informative than in the early 1950s. The neatly justified list of players' names gave not just offensive statistics but defensive ones—assists and putouts—so that you could tell from the shortstop's eight assists that the pitcher was keeping the ball low or from the left fielder's five putouts that the right-handed batters were pulling the ball and therefore that the pitches were up and not over-powering.

Not all fans read box scores this way, which is why the newspapers changed the format, but those who did felt superior to those who didn't. And the real baseball junkies learned to keep not just scorecards but the kind of records upon which box scores and all baseball statistics are based. Theoretically, at least, every significant movement can be re-corded and recovered in the kind of statistics with which even television announcers try to enliven the many dull spots of a game.

Besides, in those days most fans who followed major league baseball had to do so in print and by radio, and keeping score was a way of par-ticipating, of having memory independent of the media. Even the most hysterical radio announcers assumed that many of their listeners were keeping a complete scorebook. After describing the flurry of action in a rundown between third and home, the announcer would come down from the peak of the action with "If you're scoring, that's 5-2-6-1." In other words, or in words rather than numbers, the third baseman had thrown the ball to the catcher, who ran up the line to force the run-ner back to third where he encountered the shortstop who then threw the ball to the pitcher covering the plate, who tagged the runner for the out. The serious baseball fan would know that this was very poor strategy, since conventional wisdom is to force the runner to retreat, not advance.

The scorebook and the statistics extracted from them are obviously important, but for serious baseball fans numbers are made flesh by memory and oral history. When neither was available, imagination filled in.

The pre-eminent source of records in the 1940s and 1950s was *The Sporting News*, which carried box scores down through AA minor leagues and line scores all the way down to D, and you could follow the fortunes not only of a major league club but of its whole farm system, so that if the big club's second baseman was not hitting or making too many errors, you knew who the other second basemen in the chain were and which of them might be brought up to remedy matters. I learned about *The Sporting News* because a man who worked for my father's fruit and vegetable business about 1946 sent me to buy it at Hirsch's Drug Store, the only place in town that sold it. He couldn't go because Hirsch's also sold liquor, and the terms of his probation on a manslaughter sentence (drunk, he had shot the wrong man by mistake) barred him from entering any place that carried liquor. A very gentle man, he let me have the paper when he finished, and I was hooked for the next five years.

The Sporting News told the germ of the story of Jerry Witte. For me and for most people in Boonville, major league meant National League, but the name of the St. Louis Browns' top farm club, the Toledo Mud Hens of the American Association, caught my attention, and I began to follow the career of Witte, an outfielder. Every year, it seemed, Witte would hit thirty-eight home runs for the Mud Hens (a name I still cherish), and every spring he would be brought up to help the parent club, which needed all it could get, having a third baseman who wore glasses, for God's sake. And every year he would be sent down again to the Mud Hens. There was a moral in there that moved me but which I didn't want to examine too closely.

Many baseball fans existed in just this fashion, sustained by *The Sporting News* and *Sport Magazine* and *Baseball Digest*, making occasional pilgrimages to the nearest major league park, more often to local games for maintenance hits. Anyone who followed this pattern to its illogical conclusion wanted to stay involved with the game at any cost, even becoming a sportswriter or an umpire. And because I had a good memory and bad wrists (the eyes could be corrected), that was a path I followed until I became commissioner of my own softball league and could make a ruling, appeal it to myself, and overrule myself. The apogee came one day in Wrigley Field when, informed in highly superfluous detail about the batter's previous performance, another fan looked at my scorecard and asked if I were with the club.

Of course, all of this was only a Platonic shadow of real baseball, and more important all those years than the result was the process. I must have been six (by seven we had moved ten blocks away and I was having measles during the 1941 World Series) when I saw Donnie Viertel and another big boy playing catch in the middle of twilit Third Street, throwing it unimaginably high to be able to see it, catching it every time, a grace and completion in every exchange that must have come to an end I cannot, do not care to, recall.

By the time I could in turn be confident of catching most of what was thrown, baseball's aesthetic appeal was submerged in its social myth, which involved statistics and uniforms and chalked lines. And that myth kept us at it, provided a teleology. In those days, there was for boys under fourteen or so as little practical instruction in baseball as there was in sex. Both involved a lot of overheated imagination and a lot of individual practice, for there was no sex education in the schools (we were allowed but not taught to play baseball at recess) and there was no T-ball, Little League, or Babe Ruth League, nothing until one got to adolescence and could, if talented enough, compete with the big boys. But for anxious males on the verge of puberty, the best thing about baseball was that it had nothing to do with sex or for that matter with religion or class or any of the other puzzling matters beginning to obtrude themselves. You might not be any good at baseball, but at least you could understand it.

And you did not have to have formal coaching to play in either sense of that word. Aside from the games at recess with their well-established pecking order (right field was 9 in the scorebook and 9th in choosing up sides, and I still resent people who were never exiled there and feel unreasonably superior to those who never worked their way out) and their arguments as tense and exciting as any game, I played alone, tossing balls against the concrete front steps: sidearm to produce ground balls to backhand and short-hop; overhand snap throws which smacked against the flat and then the rise to produce popups, though never, because of some inner check, fly balls over my head; only once a full overhand throw that produced a broken window and a surprisingly mild caution from my parents, who were probably relieved that I was outdoors instead of sitting with my nose in a book. A fumbled ball did not go into any scorebook as E6, but it did interrupt the rhythm of flip and catch, left and right, up and back, more satisfying than any record of an assist. The solitary practice against the brick wall, with its thigh-high ventilation hole two bricks square, was more serious because ground balls from it, coming back across the dip of the driveway, caused me to range wider and chase farther. The hole was a target for pitching practice. Sometimes I imagined a game in which I was dramatically involved, but often it was more satisfying to concentrate on the physical process, to note the results, and to adjust the motion.

Actions not normally associated with baseball could be linked with it. Set to removing, dusting, and replacing bottles in the back room of Miller's Drug Store, I could practice pivoting on second base for double plays. Even learning to dance could be justified because it was good for footwork.

Practicing these moves was satisfying, but it was not really baseball, and there were few outlets. Occasionally a group from our Catholic school would play a team from the parish school at Martinsville, and once I organized teams of eleven-year-olds for a game at the big field in Harley Park in which I wound up catching, in glasses, without mask or pads, while Jimmy Lammers walked the bases full and then struck out the side. (I can't believe I had the nerve to do that; I couldn't believe it while I was doing it.)

Most of us got our first instruction a summer or so later when Dude Nicewarner, a wiry, sunbrowned little man in bib overalls and a rail-roader's cap, who umpired and perhaps drank a little too publicly for respectable tastes and hung about (I never did know how he made a living), somehow put out the word ("baseball" must have hung on the air like dust after a play at the plate in July) that he would be at Harley Park—the *real* baseball diamond—every afternoon and that boys could come and play. And every day, all that summer, we did. The group photo shows at least forty of us, and I am astonished that I am one of the taller players, almost as tall as Dude though shorter than Eddie Haller and thinner (as who was not?) than Max Smith, surprised to discover that I was still taking off my glasses for social occasions, and a little abashed at my precocious knowledge of how to stand out in the photo. I recognize only a few of the other boys squinting into the sun, the shorter ones on the front row shaped like children in sixteenth-century Spanish paintings, the legs all wrong, but I can taste the dust of the field behind us and feel the sweat on my back.

Every day we began with batting practice and went on to infield practice, as ritualized as, and to me more satisfying than, High Mass: ground balls hit to each player, left to right, in turn for him to throw to first base; then balls to throw to second and on to first for phantom double plays; then balls you have to charge and throw to the plate and continue running off the field and into the dugout.

In the games we had every day, I was usually put in the outfield, perhaps to get my glasses farther from the action, but I yearned to play in the infield because more was going on there and those players got to "chatter" to encourage the pitcher and daunt the opposition, and though I lacked certain physical skills, I had the lungs and larynx of a Davis. But I was happy to be playing at all, especially when I began to realize that I was more competent than some of the classmates who had ranked higher in playground status. I couldn't hit the ball very far, but most of the time I made contact, and having seen my first curveball on the narrow playground across from school, I had learned to bat left-handed in order to avoid the humiliation, worse than mere failure, of flinching from a pitch that turned out to be a strike. I discovered that cunning and forethought could make up for other deficiencies in strength and speed. I couldn't throw very hard or run very fast, but if I paid attention to where the runners were I could learn to throw to the right base, and by anticipating pitchers' and catchers' moves I could seem faster than I was. Once I worked the hidden ball trick from center field, having picked up an overthrow and held on to the ball until the runner swaggered off the base. Seeing the look on his face when I tagged him was more satisfying than getting the out. At bat in another game, I saw the catcher miss ball four and tore down the line to first, rounded it, and pulled into second with a double off a base on balls. I knew that this was possible because I had read the official baseball rules cover to cover and understood almost everything but the rules for compiling a pitcher's earned run average. Appealed to by the opposition, Dude said that I was perfectly right, and I was pleased at his tacit approval of heads-up play.

At the end of our season, as a very special privilege, we were allowed to play a game at night, under real lights, before a real crowd of parents and terminal baseball addicts. Forty years later, I do not remember any details of the game except the swarm of insects blowing toward left field (this was before DDT, and for once I was glad to wear glasses) and the sensation in my lungs and legs from chasing a hit that had crossed into foul territory. At least I was out of right field.

A year or so later, unexpectedly given a uniform and a place on the

roster of the American Legion team, I was back in right field, if I was
lucky—that is, in late innings if we were far ahead or far behind. Mostly
we were behind, losing to teams from Columbia and Jefferson City and
Sedalia. And I was an outsider, the far less competent of two Catholic
school boys who even tried out for the team. I didn't know the others
because I went to a different school, and I felt less worldly in all the
ways that increasingly mattered, less competent to deal with baseball,
sex, or any other secular matter than these boys—they can't all have
been shaving, but I remember them as appallingly mature—whose
faces and names I vaguely knew but who lived in a totally different
metaphysical world.

But at least I was learning some things I wanted to know. Kenny
Engle, the coach, had played minor league baseball and was one of the
stars of the local semipro team, the Boonville Merchants. He caught
my imagination when he failed to barehand a fly ball in left field, explaining later that his glove was full of peanuts. He was one of the few
real coaches I had in any sport and one of the best teachers because
he not only taught us how but why and when, and that on any given
play there is only one place for each player to be. You didn't have to
do anything cold; you could anticipate it, shift your feet in the field or
your hands on the bat, remind yourself where to throw a ball hit to you
depending on baserunners, outs, score. If today I were put in the outfield to catch ground balls, I would angle my legs and crouch to block
the ball as he taught me. His drills for fly balls, when he hit ball after
ball just not impossibly out of reach, were pure joy.

And while we had long suspected that how you looked was as important as what you did, Kenny taught us that the two went together. An
outfielder properly positioned to catch and throw not only looked confident, he was likely to make the right play. Naturally some of us took
mannerism for technique and spent a lot of time trying to perfect the

look of favorite ballplayers. After all, we knew of a baseball player less famous for winning the National League batting title than for taking off and putting on his hat—Harry the Hat Walker—and so we practiced striding up to the plate, adjusting our hats and any other parts of our clothing that were not quite right, spitting, planting our feet carefully, and waggling our bats at the pitcher in patterns as elaborate as a baton twirler's. Some of these actions had practical applications, especially planting the feet so that one would not fall backward in terror at a curveball, but most of them were pure ritual. We had never heard of insouciance, but we had been told of Dizzy Dean's announcement that a player had "slud nonchalantly into third," and while some of us knew that the word was used oddly, it said something important about the way real big leaguers moved and even sat.

(There was also a counter-cool tradition, embodied in Eddie Stanky, called the Brat, a sort of 1940s baseball version of John McEnroe, who substituted anger for talent, and in Enos Slaughter, a throwback to the days of Ty Cobb and filed-down spikes, but most of us were too well bred or timid to emulate them openly or consistently.)

But at game time, everything turned serious. It helped to have the moves, but you had to have the stuff. And I was not at all confident that I did. Neither were the people I played with. In Columbia, late in a losing game, an older and far more competent teammate frustrated by and distancing himself from our failure, stood ten feet away as I wavered uncertainly under a fly ball and growled, "You'd better catch it!" Later, in Jefferson City, I tried to get revenge by declining to bat for him against a pitcher who showed no sign of allowing a hit or even bat contact. My nemesis failed too, though I am not sure that he got my point.

As long as I had a uniform, I was not a total failure, but sitting on the bench denied me standing, etymologically and socially, and I could not think of myself as a real baseball player when I wasn't playing. Even when I did and the stories in the *Daily News*, written from the scorebook rather than eyewitness reports, testified to my prowess, I knew better. A batter who gets a scratch hit is traditionally told, "It'll look like a line drive in the box score tomorrow." But the player knows better. Once the *Daily* credited me with driving home two runs with a clutch hit in the ninth inning to win a game. In fact, one run had scored on a wild pitch while I was at bat, and the other scored when I hit a sure groundout to first and the first baseman threw to the plate to prevent the game-ending run rather than get the meaningless out. But the scorekeeper wasn't up to this kind of subtlety. Later, given a rare chance to start at first base because Batesy Dyer didn't feel well, I faced a left-handed pitcher and, after one try batting left-handed, switched, beat out two ground balls to the infield, and blooped a soft pop down the right field line for a triple. I also tore my uniform and a little skin on my left knee while trying to dig a throw out of the dirt, and the iodine made the wound look really grisly. An opposition runner admired my guts for playing hurt, and the *Daily* said that I had furnished the power hitting and scored the only run in another loss. Only the last detail was true, and I felt a little sheepish.

I was sure that I was a better first baseman than Batesy Dyer, but that opinion was not universally held, and anyway, I realized when Harold Gilliam moved to town—he seemed as wide as Batesy and me put together and three times as strong—that I was going to have to redefine my position.

Or find somewhere else to play it. And somehow—I cannot remember or even imagine the point of contact—I was already in touch with an outlaw, unsponsored team whose nucleus was the group of boys who carried the Kansas City *Star* in Boonville. And the hard core of this cadre was the Sartain family. I didn't know any of them personally, but almost every male in town knew them by reputation.

The Sartains were spoken of with fear if not respect. Nowadays they would be called rednecks. They were so large a family, almost a clan, that I never did get all of them straight. Their parents were grandparents at thirty-six or an equally dramatic age. They lived at the dead end of Tenth Street (where I went only to throw the *Daily News*, though not to them), cut off from the respectable world by houses (most with yards less littered than theirs) inhabited by blacks. They even associated with blacks. No one cared to test their reputation for toughness. They weren't big—Chuck, the third boy and about my age, wasn't any larger than I—but were numerous and united. The word, even among adults, was, "Fight one and fight them all."

The Sartains were the anchor points of the team. The twins Billy and Bobby, shorter than I by a head, neck, and shoulderbone and two years older, were fixtures as catcher and third baseman—Eddie Stanky types to the core. Billy blocking the plate was especially impressive: throwing aside mask, glove, and hat, clenching the ball in his fist and daring the runner to come. Chuck was at first base; D.W. and Leon, with reputations, respectively, for the greatest amiability and ferocity in the family, were adjuncts. Their father served as driver and counter-threat to drunken uncles of opposing players at out-of-town games.

But even the Sartains were not numerous enough to populate a whole team. (Some families or extended families were; box scores of town-team games listed variously initialed Woolridges, for example, against another clan.) The rest—"roster" is absurdly overstated—were so various a group that we looked like a juvenile version of a World War II platoon movie. I was the only Catholic, but I was not the only oddity. One or two boys lived with divorced mothers. Two brothers came from a family of farmers so gentlemanly that they lived in the middle of Boonville in a large brick house. Two were black, making us, as far as I know, the first integrated team in that part, or any part, of Missouri until they left to join the newly formed black junior team.

The manager of the team—I don't remember him doing much coach-ing—was Herb Klusemeyer, who walked with a rocking limp from a long-ago knee injury so severe that I didn't even want to hear about it. I don't know why he bothered with the team, which occupied his weekends for several summers, except that Herbie, Jr., was a member of the team, I think as a utility player. Herb was just what I needed in an adult. He was not threateningly successful or good-looking or strong; he never yelled; and he thought I was a baseball player.

And so were we all. After protracted and complex negotiations, we ordered and paid for our uniforms, off-white with red piping, and red caps. We must have picked them up at Hirlinger's Bookstore, which had at least as much sporting equipment as books—together the most important symbols of my fantasy life—and more stationery and office equipment than either, and which smelled like no place else in Boon-ville. It was there I bought Hardy Boy books and a Rawlings Playmaker glove, a four-fingered scoop that turned bad fielders adequate and ade-quate ones occasionally spectacular. Everyone had Rawlings or Wilson equipment; one boy had a foreign-sounding Nokona and was some-thing of a pariah in those xenophobic days.

I think we called ourselves the Boonville Red Sox, but men in the barber shops and up and down Main Street called us Klusemeyer's Alley Rats, and I was secretly proud of that because it imputed a kind of junkyard toughness that I desired and sensed in my father but did not at all feel about myself. But despite the Sartain reputation, or perhaps because of it, we had no trouble among ourselves or with other teams, even in the wilds of drunk uncle–land in Prairie Home. Once on the team, I and everyone else was a member of the extended family. More-over, the Sartains didn't have to act tough because they were so obvi-ously tough that they didn't have to worry about it, and they tolerated a physically timid middle-class kid with glasses and a big mouth (I don't know if they saw me that way, but I did) because I could catch fly balls out of my territory and use the voice to distract opposing pitchers and because I was, temporarily, with them and against the world. (When I read Tom Wolfe's accounts of the fascinating, horrifying lower classes, I had already been there. I had already read Tom Sawyer's "I stopped to play with Huckleberry Finn.") The only time they were dangerous was when I played first base and Billy dropped a third strike and threw to the foul side of first base, stretching me out in the path of the runner. But he did that to Chuck too.

The world of the team was clearly and narrowly defined. Once or twice I played catch in the Harlans' back yard, where I got the scar from sliding over a rock in a game of run-up, but that was because they lived across the street from my grandfather's bicycle shop. Otherwise we never went to each other's houses; we never hung out after games or, in the winter, after school; and we exchanged greetings but not small talk if we met on the street.

I have no idea how Herb found teams for us to play or time to go with us when we played on weekday afternoons. Nor do I have any idea how often we played. It would be impossible to find out unless Herb kept the scorebooks because we got into the papers consistently only when I started work at the Cooper County *Record* and could place the stories I was learning to write. But I can remember some of the places: Prairie Home, Tipton, New Franklin, Fayette, Armstrong, Arrow Rock. We discovered that grown-ups had told us the truth about a couple of things: the Boonville diamond had the best lights and some of the best groundskeeping (consisting mostly of a wooden drag pulled round the infield in concentric circles by a pickup truck and a regular mowing schedule). And Boonville water tasted better.

Away games were an adventure because we never knew what we would find. Arrow Rock had cow patties in the outfield. Once there was knee-high grass in New Franklin that could turn ground balls into triples and that motivated the greatest catch I ever made from center field, five feet away from the stationary right fielder whose greatest talent was getting hit by pitches, stretching out to take the ball at glove-tip just below seed-level in the ninth inning of a close game. Armstrong had single lights on each outfield foul line that made center field into a more desperate adventure than usual and a catcher who managed to throw me out only once in the seven times I tried to steal one night. Since a couple of fathers were buying a Coke for anyone who scored a run, I tended to slosh during the late innings. One Columbia field had a gigantic elm tree in dead center field. In the tenth inning, the score was tied and the competent and obnoxious pitcher, who earlier had hit me in the ass, was at the plate with a runner at third. He hit a towering fly ball that would have scored the runner against the best arm in baseball, but I was determined to deny him the satisfaction of getting a hit. I retreated past the tree to where I knew the ball would come only to hear a thwock some twenty feet up. That wasn't as bad as Fulton, where the opposition right fielder in a Legion game went back for a fly ball and disappeared into a ditch. The outfield at Prairie Home had hills and dales. Fielding grounders across the dip and gravel of the driveway was the best preparation for this kind of baseball.

Although playing teams from the Missouri Training School for Boys —certified city toughs, for whom we felt real awe, but not highly competent ballplayers—was the furthest reach of our experience, Columbia, twenty-five miles away, was the farthest we went physically. Considering our transportation, this was just as well. Herb always drove what I remember as a prewar sedan. Mr. Sartain (we always preserved the distinction) had a series of cars, including a 1940 Buick, as solid as a crypt, which we thought could go a hundred miles an hour. Later the Sartain boys were allowed to drive an old three-quarter ton International flatbed truck with racks on the side. Whoever sat next to the driver had the important task of holding the gearshift so that it would not slip back into neutral. Once or twice we had shortstops—Buddy Duel, who went on to a sectarian college with the purported end of becoming a preacher; Clifford Kateman, sharp-profiled and eastern, with better moves than hands—old enough to drive. I can't remember my parents driving or even coming to a game, which at that age was a relief. Having my own world, entirely separate from home or religion or school, was more important to me than I could formulate at the time, though I think I realized it.

One of the great things about the Alley Rats was that you got to play a lot of positions. Billy and Bobby were fixtures, but after starting out in center field I moved to first base when Chuck began playing for the Legion and a couple of times played shortstop. Since we only had two boys regarded as pitchers, I even got on the mound a couple of times. The first time, playing in New Franklin, I had no idea how to wind up and wasted a lot of motion, and it was hard for me to see baserunners beyond the scope of my glasses. But according to a clipping preserved by my grandmother, I pitched a six-hitter, not because I had a good arm—as Billy pointed out, repeatedly and with growing exasperation, he was throwing the ball out harder than I was in—but because of the control I had gained from pitching to the hole in the wall. We won easily.

Even more gratifying than the win was the sense of solidarity I felt with the Sartains. Playing for New Franklin was a Boonville boy a grade ahead of me. I guess I should have been fond of him because, though he tried to bully me, he was the only person on the playground I consistently beat in fights. But I didn't like him at all, fearing at some level that he was a kind of parody of me. Probably he felt the same way. Anyway, attempting to score from third base, he tried to run over

Billy, who tagged him out as hard as possible. Then Chuck and Bobby converged from first and third base and I joined them from the mound. None of the New Franklin boys were inclined to defend their temporary teammate, and while nothing happened, I was delighted to be on the outside of the circle for a change.

The world of the Alley Rats had little to do with adult fears and values. We would have scoffed at Grantland Rice's view that "it isn't whether you won or lost, but how you played the game" because we always wanted to win. But except for momentary chagrin at a mistake or mischance, I cannot remember being devastated by losing.

Only once did winning give me the kind of deep satisfaction I can still feel warmly. Early one season I made one more try at the American Legion team. This was not exactly treachery to Herb, who unlike the Legion coaches didn't care whether or where else someone played. I was pretty sure that I would not start and even that I might be cut, but I could not quit.

Then Dude, who by that time was coach, scheduled a practice game against the Alley Rats, who showed up without a rested pitcher. I was so obviously a spare that Dude offered to loan me for the occasion, so I moved to the third base dugout. This was more than an experiment, and I concentrated as hard as I ever had. I made some mistakes, partly because my peripheral vision was no better, partly because I lacked experience. Billy Cleary, my classmate from the Catholic school, hit for two bases the slip pitch I had invented and then stole home. But I didn't make many mental errors, and I remember, or want to remember, that we caught Billy on a second attempted steal. At the end of six or seven innings we were ahead by a comfortable margin and I was too arm-weary to shift my hat.

I was even tired enough to have the sense to tell Herb, and he told Dude. Dude hadn't held me in high regard, but he made a gallant gesture. Losing to the Alley Rats would be humiliating to the town's official team, and in offering Herb a minor utility player he must have been sure that his team would win. But when Herb told him that my arm had given out, he sent over Charlie Hirlinger, not his best pitcher but a real pitcher, who preserved my win.

My determination more than my performance—Dude was a good baseball man and knew that I had gotten by on guts rather than talent—kept me on the Legion roster, but my heart and pretty soon my body were back with Herb. I don't remember what year that was or how much longer I played for him; people say that my memory is exceptional, but those seasons blend together regardless of what happened the rest of those years. But I do know that it felt good to be an unofficial, outlaw ballplayer on a team without a schedule, unranked in standings, with no statistics kept to apportion praise or blame. By 1951 I was good enough or looked good enough to be called in, with Chuck, to play as a ringer for a team of New Franklin high school boys.

The last game I played for the Alley Rats I almost didn't. In August 1951 a team from Glasgow came to play us, and their manager insisted that no one over sixteen be used. Billy and Bobby, though eighteen, passed for less; Chuck was by that time playing for the Legion. But the Glasgow manager insisted that I had to be more than sixteen. In a way, this was gratifying, but statistically my seventeenth birthday, like my departure for college, was a month away. Having snuck in two ringers, Herb was inclined to be gracious: he would not play me unless we got behind. So Randy Meyer got to start at first base for the first time in his life. I now realize that this must have been very exciting for him, but it was very frustrating for me, after all those years of being too small and too incompetent to play, to be benched for the opposite reasons.

We did get behind, and I did get to play. What followed was not exactly pretty, but it was a suitable end to my career in outlaw ball. I reached base a couple of times, once on a high pop fly that everyone lost in the sun, but was not distinguishing myself. I can't remember what the scorebook would have said about my last at bat, in the bottom of the ninth inning, but I probably strode to the plate, stuck my bat handle up between my thighs, spat, adjusted my hat, twisted my left foot into the baked dust, placed the right foot carefully eighteen inches in front, swung the bat forward and up with my right hand, brought it back and up to put my left hand on top, took a practice swing that ended with the barrel pointed toward the pitcher, bent my knees slightly, pulled the bat back and up, lowered my hands level with my left mastoid bone, and cocked my head to the right and slightly down, staring at the pitcher from under my cap bill with what I hoped was a steely stare.

In fact, I don't remember doing this, but since it was what I always did, I would bet on it. I cannot remember or even imagine how I got to first base, but I did, and, as was usual in those days, either stole second or advanced on a passed ball. At any rate, I was still there when, with two outs, a runner ahead of me at third, and the Alley Rats one run down, the batter hit a routine ground ball toward the shortstop. I remembered having booted a ball and lost a game in New Franklin under similar circumstances, so I trotted very slowly toward third, avoided the ball, and accelerated, as it went through the shortstop's legs, to round third and score the winning run.

There was an enormous argument. The Glasgow manager raved that I should have been called out for interference, that I should not have been playing in the first place, that he would never bring another team to Boonville. He appealed to the heavens and to the umpire. We did not bother to interrupt our victory celebration; the umpire was Mr. Sartain. A little savvy right on the edge of cheating, a little speed, a little intimidation, and a lot of home field advantage: a suitable end to my Alley Rat career.

A month later I packed my glove for college, and though I used it sporadically in softball games until, in 1966, it rotted beyond repair or even nostalgia, I never tossed it negligently behind me at the end of another inning of baseball, and I never again put on a uniform. I worked out briefly with the college team, but I knew that I was not serious, and I never tried out for the Boonville Ban Johnson team for players eighteen to twenty-one. The last time I went on a field for a departmental softball game, in my early fifties, I still looked as though I knew what I was doing. But after a collision at home plate while trying to cut off the lead run, I realized that my mind was telling my body to do impossible things, and that's the last time I'll walk onto a field.

Anyway, I feel lucky to have been an Alley Rat, to have embodied, in however brief and pale a fashion, a dream. I was even luckier to realize that it was time to wake to vaguer dreams for other days.

Boys and Girls

All of us in the class of 1951 knew that something more than usually serious was up when the principal announced that Monsignor Roels would make a more than usually formal visit to the high school to talk to the seniors. Boys and girls separately. We knew that this meant SEX, and though by this time most of us knew something about the theory and a few of us had had some practice, official word from an adult and ecclesiastical, though celibate, source made most of us feel a little uncomfortable. Nuns might talk about purity, but as adolescent males, we had learned not to pay much attention to them. When priests talked about sex, mostly in the confessional and then only if provoked, the matter was serious.

We may have thought—I certainly did—that from an adult point of view we had been almost as guilty in our innocence as in our practice. We all knew the official church line that we had been wrong in whatever we were doing. Furthermore, those of us on the boys' basketball team remembered watching the first half of the girls' games before going downstairs to suit up and ping-ponging a running joke about the sudden and localized weight gain by one of the girls. It turned out to be no joke. She had named as father a boy who had graduated two classes ahead of us, and, rumor went, her nominee had brought to the rectory a half-dozen others, including two of my classmates, who confessed to having had sex with her. In the male folklore of the time, that was enough to convict her of being a "common prostitute." However the scenario went, she left school and town abruptly. We were pretty sure that the heat from that would scorch even the innocent because we had guilty impulses even if, in this case or in this manner, we hadn't acted on them.

Before the monsignor arrived, we were already seated in the room usually devoted to English classes. As if to underscore the strangeness of the situation, each of us chose a seat different from every other day. There was no horseplay and only a little nervous display of bravado.

The monsignor didn't just come in. He made an entrance. Tall as any of us and a lot more stately, gray hair with a bald spot making an involuntary tonsure, cassock (like an ankle-length dress buttoned all the way down) with the violet piping and buttons of his rank, he looked as serious as Jehovah handing over the tablets.

I remember the room and the spring day—the sun was shining through the south windows—and almost exactly where I sat, about halfway back in the room and two or three rows away from my usual seat by the window. But I remember only one thing from the talk, perhaps because it was necessarily vague if it was not going to be inflammatory.

He warned us of the danger of attending the nearby University of Missouri not only because it was a secular school and thus technically off limits to Catholics but also because, he said, "I doubt that there is a single virgin enrolled in that school." (We never found out what he said to the girls because none of us had the nerve to ask any of them.)

We knew that the monsignor was a good man and a concerned pastor who had been grieved and shocked by the sin from which the pregnancy resulted. We also knew that he was a man of wide learning and surprising good sense. So it may seem astonishing that he would regard the virgin shortage as a serious deterrent.

Something even more astonishing: it did worry some of us. The prospect of losing our faith or falling into mortal sin—we knew what to do about that—was less daunting than the prospect of having to deal with girls who knew what to do when we didn't. I felt very nervous at the prospect of encountering girls who were not virgins because I had never, to my knowledge, associated with any.

In fact, girls who presumably were virgins were hard enough to figure out because, except for time spent in class, where they got along a lot better than the boys did because they were neat and tidy and had the nuns on their side, they had always seemed to live in a culture and even a world entirely separate from ours. They washed a lot more, or more effectively, than we did. They had a different and more socially accept-able vocabulary. And they obviously lived in a different moral universe. At daily mass from the first grade on, they were separated from us by the wide center aisle. Spiritually, the gulf seemed a lot wider. Accord-ing to the precepts we were taught, girls were temples of the Holy Ghost and therefore had an inside track on the virtue of purity. They were vested with control over . . . well, not their impulses, since officially they didn't have any, but over any sticky situations that might arise in their dealings with boys. The triple deterrents of the old limerick all operated, especially the first and third:

> *There was a young lady name Wilde*
> *Who kept herself quite undefiled*
> *By thinking of Jesus*
> *And contagious diseases*
> *And the bother of having a child.*

Actually, the precepts of the church taught that boys were also tem-ples of the Holy Ghost, but since we were the official menace to female purity, we could see that not even the nuns really believed that, and we had increasingly frequent and often embarrassing reminders that the Holy Ghost's jurisdiction was limited. So was the power of our own wills. As one of my contemporaries put it ruefully, "I wish I could just tell it to lie down, and it would."

We were so convinced of our own depravity that we had discovered only a couple of months before Monsignor Roels's talk that "virgin" was not a sex-specific term. During the annual school retreat (a kind of Catholic version of a revival; see the third chapter of James Joyce's *A Portrait of the Artist as a Young Man* for a full-dress version), the visiting priest had asked for written questions. One of the slower and more ingenuous boys—ingenuous enough to admit that it was his question— wanted to know if a boy could be a virgin, and the priest delivered a brief homily on the value of purity for boys as well as girls. The boy who asked the question may have believed him, but while the rest of us could follow the theory, we all knew on a basic level that virginity in males was an absence of experience, which some of us knew that we didn't have and weren't really sure we'd ever have.

We didn't even know how much we didn't know because there was a lot less information available to us than kids have today, even about basic physiology. The most explicit material widely available was the lingerie section of a mail-order catalog, and the illustrations there would seem tame by the standards of today's Sears catalog. This was before undergarments or photographers would admit that women had nipples. Dance sequences in movies were exciting because the women's skirts would twirl out to reveal their thighs and what looked to the unpracticed eye like panties (also called step-ins, which sounded a lot sexier), though it was hard to think of Vera-Ellen, Ann Miller, or June Allyson, who played various versions of the girl-next-door, as sexy. Cyd Charisse was another matter.

Occasionally we got hold of soft-porn magazines printed in black and white on cheap paper featuring mostly back views of crouching adult women who seemed grotesquely misproportioned for any purposes we could imagine or desire. Sexuality seemed harsh and brutish, part of the sleazy backstreet atmosphere of the *True Confession* magazines that baby-sitters and beauty operators read or of the language we heard in locker-room jokes and bragging from older boys and tried to use correctly before we had any physical referent for them. (The techniques guaranteed to drive women wild with desire we could not comprehend, and those we did we couldn't imagine ourselves actually doing with any girl we were likely to meet.) We didn't see any filtered, air-brushed breast and crotch shots. We never heard any other language for love or romance that any sensible kid would use. Nothing we heard or saw seemed to have anything to do with the girls in our classes.

Moving pictures were even less helpful. Like the characters in Mordecai Richler's *Cock-Sure* and Woody Allen's *Purple Rose of Cairo*, we could see what happened until the first kiss (mouth closed, at least one foot each on the floor, even married couples safely separate in twin beds), but all scripts called for a fade-out long before any clothing was deranged. In the movies, the girl's raising one foot in the middle of an embrace was a sign that she was really in love with the man, but most of us knew nothing about the physiological effects of that movement and anyway couldn't have believed that any girl we were likely to encounter would have that equipment or those impulses.

Books could be more satisfactory than pictures, moving or not, because I could project into them my own confused emotions and desires. I don't mean books regarded as "hot," like *Forever Amber*, *The Strumpet Wind*, *The Queen's Physician*, or other middlebrow stroke material that came from some of the book clubs, though at a later stage they offered rudimentary instruction in the physical and verbal techniques of seduction. I mean Edgar Rice Burroughs. Not so much the Tarzan books, though they had their moments, as the ones featuring John Carter, the Virginia gentleman who somehow got to Mars. He was better than cowboys because he could not only ride and shoot, having been a Confederate cavalryman, but he was an expert swordsman and could fly or drive or ride anything that moved and learn any language in three pages flat. Besides, in the lower gravity of Mars, his earth conditioning made him a supra-martian if not a superman. He killed bad Indians— sorry, six-limbed, eight-foot green barbarians—and made friends with good ones like Tars Tarkas and his tribe, the off-world equivalent of Tarzan's Waziri.

John Carter was obviously made from the same template as Tarzan, with spoilers and more chrome, but he stirred my imagination more. Tarzan was always being coveted by exotic women who wanted— recognizing white Anglo-Saxon aristocratic superiority—to improve the breed or just fool around, and in the original Tarzan book Burroughs hints (broadly enough to get the point across even to inexperienced adolescents) that Tarzan and Jane are not a little excited by the prospect of some interspecies miscegenation. The occasional ape male—and lesser breeds like Slavs and Latins, all of whom said "Sapristi!"—might lust after a white woman if her clothing were picturesquely disordered. Black villains were innocent of these desires.

In the Tarzan books, this motif was muted; in the Tarzan movies, it was plugged. But in the John Carter books, it was right up front with full brass. Deja Thoris, the Martian princess and lead heroine, lays eggs that can be fertilized by an earthling. She also has red skin and a really great figure. Burroughs isn't very explicit about the finer points, but the idea is inescapable. She is continually being tied up and drooled over by lustful males from a surprising variety of species and colors. Then John Carter climbs, drops, sneaks, or charges in with his long sword to kill the villain, set her free, and receive her gratitude and later an egg or two for the hatchery. All of this played to my private soundtrack of

Perry Como's version of "Temptation": "You were born to be kissed, /
I can't resist. / You are temptation / and I am yours."

It was all there: the strangeness, the attraction, even fascination,
the promise of an ultimate union whose details were unimaginable
with a female unlike the familiar Penelope or even Jane but as exotic
as any being the wandering male encountered during his adventures.
Burroughs's zoology may have been a little off—carnivorous apes, for
example—but his sexual psychology seemed dead accurate to the adolescent mind.

(Not long ago I found at a garage sale a paperback of one of the John
Carter books, paid my quarter, and took it home to see if it had the
same charge. In this one, Deja Thoris was pretty much just a wife, to
be cherished and rescued and all that, but it seemed a lot less exciting,
even to John Carter, to rescue a wife than to snatch a virgin from the
dripping fangs of a menace who made your own awful desires seem
chaste by comparison.)

Meanwhile, in real life as distinct from what we learned in church,
school, and visual and narrative art, females did not seem to need much
rescuing. For one thing, until late junior high school, they were bigger than most of us, and socially they had a lot more savvy. The nuns
didn't belt them around. When we became aware of them as female,
they seemed to have all the power, in fact as well as in theory. They
could just say no and make it stick. The only hint that this might be
reversed was the dust jacket of a paperback I saw in Foster's Drug Store
but never read. It showed a well-groomed, clearly aristocratic man in
a dressing gown seated in a chair with a woman sprawled on the floor
and clinging to his knee. John Carter was a lot more believable.

But all that was theory, slowly accumulated and painfully assimi-
lated, and it could be kept at an uneasy distance. Real girls presented
increasing difficulties. And for a while the ones who implied that they

might say yes before we knew what that meant presented greater problems than the ones who could only say no. It was obvious that they knew what they were doing even if it wasn't clear why they wanted to do it, or what it was.

The first seductive female I encountered must have been about twelve to my nine or ten. We were both visiting Otterville. She was a preacher's daughter and therefore a Protestant, and she talked in an arch and knowing way, telling the first dirty joke I had ever heard from a girl—using "frying steak" as a euphemism for intercourse with the punch line, "It must be done, 'cause I can feel the gravy running down my leg"—and suggesting vague and portentous emotional connections between us. She seemed as exotic as Deja Thoris. And me too young to have a sword.

The official view seemed to be that children—kids as well as little kids—did not have sexual impulses, and it was so strongly engrained that when I first read Freud on infant sexuality, I wondered uneasily who had been monitoring my thoughts. At ten, I didn't think much, but I certainly felt the power of the sensations she evoked.

The girls in Boonville were less threatening, even when I reached puberty, because encounters with them were controlled by a code of behavior that we established ourselves. At the swimming pool, for example, it was permissible to talk to girls and even to hang around them in a vague sort of way, but until you were so big a kid that you were almost an adult, you didn't hang out *with* them. The same thing was true of the soda fountains. I don't remember what we said to them. Mostly we just cast what we hoped were unperceived glances at deepening cleavages. (Most adolescent girls had at least some cleavage—a subsecondary sexual characteristic that seems to have disappeared from the language. A study of old movies and pin-up photos and even Wonder Woman comics—the only sources of information I had—will show that the technology of the brassiere was a lot different in those days.)

To get a really good look, you had to get up close, and this meant that you had to be presentable enough to be allowed within ogling distance. This wasn't terribly difficult as long as you washed with some frequency and combed your hair and didn't use really filthy language like "damn" or "hell," let alone anything scatological. In short, behave as the grown-up world taught us, on the official theory that girls were most impressed by gentlemanly, respectful boys.

Like most adult theories, this could get you by, but our observations showed us that it wouldn't really get you anywhere. The boys who got close enough to touch as well as look were hardly models for Catholic or any smalltown youth. They smoked and drank and used questionable language and were anything but deferential to girls. On the other hand, they could dance well and move with the kind of feline panache later demonstrated by James Dean. If they were really feckless, they seemed to appeal to girls who were supposed to know better but who seemed to think that it was their mission to apply the love of a good woman and bring these wanderers back to the fold. This seemed to us grossly unfair. For one thing, my friends and I couldn't jitterbug, as we still called it, and we didn't know where to learn, except in public, which was too humiliating to think about. Besides, we were still a little scared of girls who knew how to do those dances, all from the public school. Anyway, except for some abortive attempts to start a teen center in response to the perennial complaint that there was nothing for us to do in Boonville, we didn't go to places where they danced that way.

On the other hand, the Catholic school did sponsor dances, starting with the seventh and eighth grade (a lot of one-on-one mismatches there), and most of the boys learned to dance because that was the only socially acceptable way you could touch a girl. One of us did just like to dance and achieved professional status, but later developments proved, as we had long suspected, that his interest was purely aesthetic. These dances were heavily chaperoned and so leadenly decorous that there was not much to deter.

There were also hayrides. The less you know about hay, the more romantic that sounds. We had seen hayrides in movies, but somehow ours never attained that romantic aura. Besides, no one in the movie ever had his mother along. Mom was popular as chaperone because she would drive the truck or tractor and leave us to any devices that we could imagine in the crowded wagon bed sprawled on prickly and dusty hay. Mom professed not to understand my objections not because she was trying to cramp my style (I didn't have any) but because she liked to drive.

Parents became less visible as we got older, especially at home parties where we danced a little, made popcorn, drank Cokes, played games, and acted like supporting actors in a June Allyson movie until one of the more daring parents not only allowed but actively encouraged kissing games. (This and subsequent experience showed that Catholic girls got really good at kissing because very modest experiments in that genre, lips closed but not rigid, were right at the borderline of moral acceptability, so they could practice without feeling terribly guilty.) The boys didn't know how most of the girls felt about it—the daughter of the daring mother quite openly enjoyed it—because we never asked them. We may have felt that the less they noticed, the better for us. I think they had been trained to believe that the less they officially noticed, the better for them, but that is speculation because we didn't spend much time talking to them about this or about anything else. I can reconstruct the costumes (lots of white bucks and bobby sox and plaid skirts) and background music (Nat Cole and a lot of really boring white singers who sounded very much alike), but I can't remember any dialogue. Maybe that is because nothing was being said.

By the time I was a senior in high school, things got a little more relaxed, and not just because Mom ignored the fact that some of the boys were bringing alcohol to parties at our house. In fact, nobody seemed stiff in any sense, even the time when one pedantic junior wrote "4/5 quart Mogen David" on the shopping list and a senior unused to fine distinctions got six fifths just to be on the safe side. We may have been more comfortable around girls because all of us were thinking about something else for a change. Everybody knew which of us would be leaving for college or nurses's training or for jobs at the edge of the earth in Kansas City or St. Louis, and girls as well as boys lived more in anticipation of new places and people than in the present. Those of us who "dated," and they were not in the majority, tended to seek out girls in the sophomore class who were more attractive in conventional ways and were not too far beyond us in social development. This seemed to be nothing more than practice on either side. Our classmates were not exactly taboo, but they didn't seem appropriate or available as objects of desire because we knew each other too well. Besides, as the senior year wore on, they became more like comrades than like females because we were all about to venture out of Boonville. The process of learning about sex and romance and, if we were lucky, love occurred in other times and places.

I don't know if males still grow up suspecting that females belong to a different and probably alien species—a view that some feminists seem disinclined to dispel—because I had few opportunities to observe my children's social development and paid as little attention as I could. I suspect that, what with peer pressure and explicit sexuality in all kinds of media, they had more experience earlier than I did. I do know that my children seemed to find it possible to be friends with members of the opposite sex a couple of decades earlier than I did. They have had roommates—not a euphemism, they say and I believe—of the opposite sex. They are getting engaged and married, or not, later than I did.

Perhaps they have been spared some of the misconceptions and will avoid some of the mistakes.

Only my son ever asked me for advice. He was a little oblique partly because that's the way he is but mostly because he had some evidence that I was having less trouble than he in approaching women. He wanted me to tell him what I never thought my father knew or needed to know and never got around to explaining to me: how to deal with women. The only thing I could think of was a secret that my education and conditioning had concealed and that it had taken me years to learn: like human beings.

So far, he hasn't reported back on how that works. Maybe he will in twenty years or so.

Art and Life

There wasn't much Art in Boonville, but not many people objected because, as far as we could tell, the purpose of Art was to do you good even if it made you uncomfortable. In fact, the less comfortable you were, apparently, the more good it did you. My mother used this line of reasoning to justify serving liver and urging me to read *David Copperfield*.

Capital Art was official: classical music and what used to be called semiclassical (and is now called elevator music) on the radio and on phonographs in houses where none of my friends lived; the readings assigned in English class—Hawthorne, Scott, Dickens, Shakespeare, assorted very dead poets; the books that the librarian suggested in order to try to convert a gormand into a gourmet reader; movies if they had Shakespeare or religion in them—the Catholic school kids were taken to see *The Song of Bernadette* during Lent, an exception to the iron-clad rule which, we felt, must have required direct papal dispensation; magazines without pictures; Book-of-the-Month Club offerings.

With rare exceptions, mostly female, Art was a consumer product. In school, the perfunctory art lessons were even more torturous than arithmetic because I couldn't draw a lick, not even, when I got to college, a satisfactory amoeba for biology class. But then nobody worked very hard at drawing. The only association for the word "studio" would have been "photography." Music classes were more fun, especially when we got old and bold enough to agitate the nun in charge, and some of us had music lessons that taught us rudimentary skills without indicating that music might have anything to do with form or feeling. We had dances, but no Dance. If there was a dance studio in town, I never heard of it. We had school plays—why, I now wonder. Was there a rationale, or did the administration just do it because that is what schools did? Books could be Art, but writing was a skill that might become a trade, like building: the point was to hammer things together so that they would stand up. I had heard the term "architect" before I left Boonville only because an older cousin in New Mexico had become one. She could also paint—we had one of her watercolors on our livingroom wall—and this seemed every bit as exotic.

People who consumed Art—who had "acquired culture," a later way of putting it—were superior to people who didn't. They weren't as funny or as interesting or as normal, but they belonged to a different caste. (One near contemporary was what we hadn't yet learned to call "arty." There was some talk of forming a boy's club which he wanted to call the "Trocadero." But then he kept guppies and later became a dancer and model.) Most of us were pleased with the difference because it meant that Art could be something that other people did while the rest of us could go on being normal. Sort of like Life, which was what grown-ups did.

In other words, the concept of Art took a lot of pressure off us and the things we experienced every day. For example, we didn't have the concept of vernacular architecture, but Boonville did have a lot of brick buildings that we knew were old and that were handsomer and more impressive-looking than the new ones. We didn't have a movement to preserve or list them on a historic sites map (one was issued thirty years later by the Friends of Historic Boonville), but cultural lag, inertia, family loyalty, and stinginess worked almost as well and a lot less obtrusively. If we had been made to study and honor them, we would probably have paid less real attention.

You had to pay attention in church, or at least act like it, and the furnishings and some parts of the ritual—I don't think anybody thought of them as Art—were a real relief. The Catholic church (the old, semigothic one, not the new one that looks like something run up for deritualized Congregationalists) may not have had the only stained glass in town, but it was the only stained glass I saw from the inside, and during a long and abstruse sermon or an interminable "Gloria in excelsis Deo" I could focus on one color after another or trace the patterns made by the leads. I think that the church did have the only statues in town until some organization paid for the miniature Statue of Liberty or whatever it is that now stands in front of the courthouse. The expressions on the faces of the holy family and the saints implied a pleasant contrast to the assumptions about our depravity being voiced from the altar or pulpit. Even the vestments, in different shapes and colors, with something like luxury in their fabrics and art in their decoration, were different from everyday.

The language of the church services—translated, of course; not half a dozen people in town could follow it in Latin—was also removed from everyday. The epistles and gospels, from the Douay translation of the Bible, weren't as elegantly Elizabethan as those in the King James version, but the sentences had a vocabulary and, more important, a cadence we heard nowhere else. When the unjust steward in the parable faced an audit, he didn't say something like, "Oh, my God! I'm finished!" Instead, in perfectly balanced clauses, he reflected, "To dig I am unable; to beg I am ashamed." I had never heard anybody talk like that, especially a man in shit that deep. But the good guys, even God, talked at least as well. Randolph Scott couldn't have outdone in understatement the landowner who looks at his field full of thistles and says, no doubt with eyes slitted, "An enemy hath done this." True, the disciples often sounded like stooges, but it was consoling to realize that even saints could make stupid remarks and, still better, be forgiven for them.

The music was a very mixed blessing. The blue hymn books in the choir loft contained a number of treacly pious hymns to the Virgin Mary either written or arranged by Nicolai A. Montini. That name under a title oppressed the heart because we knew that the sentiments would be saccharine and the tunes, spread across several octaves, unsingable. The "Mass of the Angels" sung at High Mass wasn't much better—repeating "gloria" thirty-seven times wasn't anywhere near as stimulating as the "come, come, come" of "Church in the Wildwood," which had put an end to the boys' chorus in high school—but the songs for Benediction, especially the "Tantum Ergo," with lyrics by another Italian named St. Thomas Aquinas, had a real drive to them no matter which arrangement was used. And Gregorian chant was not only singable but direct and to the point. It was regrettable when someone died, but at least we got to sing the requiem mass and the "Dies Irae," which was less reassuring but more sensible than "Daily, daily, sing to Mary," at least until, after the vernacularization of the mass in the sixties, it was translated into tetrameter triplets that made it sound like a toothpaste commercial.

Even if it had sounded that way then, we were not supposed to notice. It was like hearing of a wicked or careless priest ("stupid" was not a possible category, though "boring" was acceptable if the word itself wasn't used): you were supposed to respect the office rather than pay attention to the human being filling it. And the pious object was to be valued because of what it aimed at rather than what it accomplished. Substance—well, content—was everything. Style was nothing. Virtue was not its own reward. A highly colored holy card from Sister was the reward.

This was such obvious bullshit that we wouldn't have bothered to argue about it even if we had dared. In fact, we were starved for style and consequently suckers for stylization. Fortunately, Art and whatever went on in church and school did not exhaust the categories. There was also Trash, now spoiled for everybody by being termed popular culture, which included anything that a normal boy might want to listen to, look at, or read. Trash included all comic books, most radio shows, virtually all movies, and, should anyone admit to reading at all, books with an interesting plot. The comics were absolutely shameless; every other character seemed to wear a mask or have incredible super powers that enabled him to fly higher, swim faster, stretch farther than normal human beings, and the more outrageous they were, the more we reveled in them. Plastic Man was one of my favorites because he was not only ridiculous, he had a sense of humor about his powers and himself. When the boy sidekick of the Spirit wanted to murder and mayhem the bad guys and was told that he couldn't do both, he said, "OK, then we'll murder them and mayhem their bodies." This was a refreshing change from the gee-whiz style of Robin and others.

Movies were tied a bit closer to reality or at least to possibility, but style was character, all the way from Errol Flynn's tights to the silk scarf fluttering behind the leather jackets and helmets of the Flying Tiger aces and the elaborate costumes and sets of the movie musicals, down to the B westerns we saw every Saturday in a double feature where the best people had the neatest-looking horses and got to ignore the surviving if not the most exciting women in the cast. And we made strict and inflexible distinctions. I still don't trust the judgment of anyone who prefers Gene Kelly to Fred Astaire, because while my light-footed friend was the only person who ever wore a turtleneck in Boonville, nobody at all wore white tie and tails. Besides, Astaire had enough sense to come in out of the rain, preferably into a modest living room forty or fifty yards square.

Still, there were limits. Roy Rogers was outside the pale because he dressed too funny and looked too pretty. Gene Autry's costume was a little more suited to the range, but he too had an incurable tendency to burst into song. We began to notice that the hero's six-shooter held more rounds than a P-51 fighter's belts and to suspect that fanning a gun was not likely to produce significant results without major help from the scriptwriter. But it took a little effort to adjust even to the vestiges of surface realism. When I first saw a movie in which the hero (Johnny Mack Brown) cocked and fired a single-action revolver, I thought something was wrong with his gun.

Comics and movies and many of the books we read offered us an escape from what we feared we were in everyday life—timid, weak, not very athletic or attractive or able to deal with things or people. (I'm talking about myself, of course, but all that consoling compensatory myth couldn't have been directed just at me.) But it became increasingly obvious that we were going to have to deal with them. One day, after a matinee of *The Desert Song*, I galloped toward home on an imaginary Arab steed to the accompaniment of a Sigmund Romberg tune, more exalted than I had ever been in church or anywhere else. Just after I turned from Walnut Street hill to the flat stretch of Third Street, it was as if my mind split and even at the age of twelve I realized that, magnificent, desirable, and even, at one level, accessible as the movie world might be, it wasn't life. I might become a baritone, but I was no more likely to become a superb horseman than I was to develop piercing eyesight. And, I realized, it was OK. I could live with that.

Although I continued to go to movies, they offered, and I expected, less compensation. The ones that now impressed me more than I could say, even to myself, struck a note of melancholy. In 1950, when I was turning sixteen, *The Gunfighter* appeared, the first western adult enough to show that gunfighters could have angst too, that you couldn't always ride away from complication or back into a life you had thrown away, that the west could be mean and shabby and the clothes grimy, that movies and life did not have to end in physical and moral victory. (*High Noon* and *Shane*, which came along two years later, implied that it did, which is probably why these movies have been a lot more popular than *The Gunfighter*.)

Even horror movies began to take on a new edge. Not those featuring the classic, inhuman menaces from the 1930s, which by this time had been taken over by Abbott and Costello farces, but the ones in which the monster, who began as human, recognized and was horrified by his own change, and sought vainly to reverse it. The Wolf Man movies were in this genre, but even more striking to me was one (whose title and actors I can't remember) in which the central character survives a lightning bolt only to discover that he has an insatiable craving for electricity, that the natural world he loves is repelled by him, and that his newly acquired superhuman powers bring him no pleasure or consolation. Like the wolf man or Johnny Ringo in *The Gunfighter*, he can rejoin humanity only in death.

There was a kind of melancholy satisfaction in observing the fates of characters different from everybody around them because, of course, I thought nobody but me was different from everybody, and I longed for a world in which I wasn't. This wasn't something you talked about—though you could hint at it for brief moments with particularly close friends—because introspection and self-consciousness were not highly valued.

Books were more suspect than movies because they were a completely private indulgence. As a matter of fact, reading, at least for pleasure, was widely regarded as downright antisocial and might even make hair grow on your palms. On the other hand, it was possible to have a marginally enviable reputation as a good reader, and since I blew the top off every reading test the nuns gave me, I was known, or notorious, as a top hand with a book. And like the evil gunfighter in *Shane*, I was not just good at what I did. I really enjoyed it. My mother used to say that I would rather read than eat.

This talent, or obsession, wasn't much of an advantage in real life. It did allow me to flip through more comic books than most people at the drugstore newsstand before Frank Foster ran me off. In school, it did buy me a lot of free time and a little indulgence, since the nuns could count on me to have read the assignment or at least have scanned it for the necessary facts. I can't remember a thing from English classes except everybody trying not to giggle when Lady Macbeth says, "Unsex me. Stoppest thou the milk from my flowing breasts." There was a lot of grammar drill and memorizing and reciting, but nothing like discussion of form or even content of stuff that was supposed to be Art and, as they say in Oklahoma, sure wasn't anything else. We were given few writing assignments, though I did supply doggerel verse for most of the senior class the one time we were supposed to do something creative.

At home, books were a natural part of the furniture. My mother was a compulsive reader like her father, though her taste ran more to fiction, his to history and practical arts, and my father's older sisters were readers. Nanelou sent me books every Christmas and birthday, including *The Jungle Book*, which was the first book without pictures I read through to the end and immediately began all over again. Cary gave us a subscription to the *Reader's Digest* every year for Christmas, and though not rare, the magazine was by no means usual in the homes I visited. (In the family dichotomy, Dad wasn't supposed to be a reader. The only book he ever urged on me, after Mom died, was James

Michener's *Hawaii*, which he admired because of all the facts it contained. As he eased into retirement in his late sixties, I would visit him to find stacks of mystery stories from the local library, which he finally exhausted. When I brought him George V. Higgins's *The Friends of Eddie Coyle*, shelved with novels rather than mysteries, he balked at it on the grounds that it was "nothing but a lot of nasty talking.")

Mom belonged to a couple of book clubs, and Grandpa seemed to have his books already. I collected the Hardy Boys and ignored Nancy Drew. Hirlinger's stocked Tarzan books but not the ones featuring John Carter. Paperbacks were just beginning to show up in the drug stores, but nothing I wanted to read was being published.

The public library was my real connection to the world of books. Partly because it was located in the northeast corner of the first floor of the Cooper County Courthouse, it seemed removed from everyday life. The air was cooler in the summer; the gleaming corridors were quiet; the place smelled like nowhere else (except, when I paid a speeding ticket in 1984 in Paducah, Texas, the Cottle County Courthouse and every other one like it); and the floor-length urinals in the men's room across the hall seemed tall enough to swallow me up when I started going there.

Because the library was in the courthouse, visits seemed semiofficial and, though Jessie Dedrick, the assistant librarian, was Catholic, entirely secular. I never saw schoolmates there, and I encountered only a few public school kids, and most of them girls. Seldom any men.

I knew, without thinking much about it, that I had a certain kind of status there because I checked out so many books and went through them so fast that the elderly chief librarian exempted me from the usual limit. The status wasn't portable, as I discovered when I spent the summer at my grandparents' house in Evansville. The local library was trying to encourage children to read with a contest associated with baseball. I never bothered to figure out the rules because I didn't need any encouragement, and anyway, the librarians wouldn't believe that I was actually reading those armloads of books I carried in and out every few days and devoured on Grandma's porch swing. Besides, though I always needed a boost to my self-esteem, this was too easy to be satisfying.

The only drawback to the Boonville library was that the librarians began to take an interest in my reading and tried to shift me from the juveniles over to the adult stacks. They seemed particularly concerned, though more puzzled than distressed, by my habit of rechecking the same books. (They weren't monitoring me, but in those days, you still signed your name to the card in each book, and there weren't all that many books or patrons to keep track of.) But the adult books sounded like work or, worse, like school. Besides, the books they recommended had narrow margins and small print, and it must have been about this time that I formulated my definition of an immoral book as anything over three hundred pages long.

However, I had already begun to realize in Evansville that some books were, if not exactly immoral, disturbing in ways that I didn't want to admit or, literally, to confess. I must have got hold of some late Victorian fantasy—I seem to remember line drawings of Beardsleyesque fauns—and the atmosphere was faintly sexual and sinister in ways that seemed to have nothing to do with the incomprehensible injunctions against adultery or coveting one's neighbor's wife (why, I wondered, would anyone bother?) I encountered in sermons and catechism class. Books could be about something you couldn't share or even name.

This came to seem true of much of the really high-level trash, or, as it would now be called, adolescent literature, most of it in clearly defined genres, which I associate with the hallway outside the main room of the Boonville library. There I found Burroughs's John Carter books.

There were also various series of books devoted to sports, like the one featuring Left End Edwards and running alliteratively across the line and through the backfield, using purely WASP names, by some writer whose name I can't remember and who was probably a conglomerate anyway. The conflicts in these were external and avoidable, featuring gamblers, refractory or dishonest teammates, wish-fulfillment fantasies for boys who wanted to believe that all obstacles could be overcome and that you didn't have to go on living after the climax.

A few years later, I discovered that sports stories could actually be about something. It must have been a magazine from school that contained a story in which the star basketball player at a Catholic high school fails his teammates in the championship game because he has been weakened by what was obviously the clap. (I swear to God I'm not making this up. In those days, urban Catholics were stereotyped as the best basketball players.) Even more impressive, though still not officially literature in the eyes of the librarians, were the baseball novels of John R. Tunis—now back in print—which were obviously the work of a real writer who knew a lot about baseball and a good deal about people. The first book I read was a revelation. It featured a shortstop, Spike, and his younger brother Bobby, a second baseman. They both make the Brooklyn Dodger roster, and Spike is named player-manager at an absurdly young age, but Bobby is on the verge of being cut because, though the incumbent is almost old enough to be a pitcher, he is an established player. Spike has to deal with some of the conflicts, personal and racial (anti-Semitism), to be found in any organization. In Tunis, people age, have career-threatening injuries, deal with failure and inadequacy, go to war, and have to recuperate physically and psychically. There was a world outside Ebbetts Field and there was an inner world. Both affected what happened between the white lines. Though the naysayers never prevailed, they weren't portrayed as totally wrong or villainous. But the good guys, and the Dodgers, always won—unlike the

1946 and 1951 play-offs (forty years later, I still don't even like to hear the name Bobby Thomson) and the 1941, 1947, 1949, and 1952 World Series.

At least as impressive was the series about the adventures of Red Clark, a young gunfighter, written by Gordon R. Young. They weren't official books either, but they made it onto the library shelves, the covers literally hanging by a thread, when I discovered them. Finally they got too battered to circulate and were too lowbrow to rebind, and they disappeared from the shelves of the Boonville Public Library and, as far as I have been able to discover in forty years of intermittent searching, everywhere else in the English-speaking world.

The Red Clark books had a lot in common with B movies: the essentially upright and supercompetent gunfighter whose actions and motives are misunderstood; the self-contained adventure that was only one of a series in which the character never aged, never tired, and never developed in any way. But the books were also different. They taught me that the west was not all purple sage and glowing sunsets; that competence in one area, including gunfighting, did not automatically prepare one to cope with all emergencies and problems; that one had to learn how to look as well as be able. Two scenes remain vivid after four decades: a shabby western town battered by a sandstorm; a fight in a darkened room where Red kneels until he sees, in the flashes of gunfire, an older ally standing to do battle and rises to fight honorably. You could play cowboys with friends using material from the movies, but you couldn't play Red Clark material or even try to share it, though you could try to adopt an outward manner that expressed or at least implied the private feeling.

This was harder to do with music, but as we began to develop private tastes, we had trouble sharing those too. Group singing at parties leaned heavily toward barber shop material and Tin Pan Irishry. Current popular music tended to be solo material, and I didn't want to sound like Guy Mitchell or any of the hit singers I heard. The jazz that some of us were beginning to hear, like Dizzy Gillespie's bop lyrics, was too obscure or complicated for most tastes and larynxes.

None of us cared about Art, and it was getting less possible to share Trash. But adolescent males could find common ground in Filth.

In our more tolerant or analytic age, Filth is probably referred to as the "orally transmitted folklore of a male youth subculture," and probably attracts dissertations about regional variations in the ballad of Lil and Piss-Pot Pete (refrain: "Forty pounds of swinging meat, and stink? God DAMN!"). We didn't think about it; we just did it. Boys who wouldn't be caught dead memorizing Longfellow could spout with no effort at all whole sagas, and sometimes we would take turns, going word by word without faltering, to see who would get stuck with saying the dirtiest ones. Joke-telling sessions were useful less for the content (we had begun to develop other if not more reliable sources of information) than for the style, and by our mid-teens we were more interested in stepping on someone's lines or undercutting his style than we were in hearing the punchline. Timing, surprise, and a growing sense of what has to be called form became more important. We were delighted with a contemporary's discovery of a new dirty song, beginning "There once was a bird no bigger than a turd," that, I realized, could be turned into a round-song, like "Row, row, row your boat" or some of the other vapidities foisted on us in music class.

I think at some level we recognized that this stuff was not, like Trash, a form of escape but a form of attack on all kinds of official pieties. And some of us began to understand dimly that there were alternatives to the Art and Trash provided us and that they might offer literal as well as imaginative escape. I saw the first issue of *Mad Comics* at Foster's Drug Store, opened it to see a gross, accurate, and very funny parody of Superman, and felt for the first time that here was an enthusiasm I could share with my contemporaries because it mocked our almost-abandoned idols as well as those of the dominant culture, like the parody of *Reader's Digest* that carried the subtitle, "Articles Lacking in Interest." Of course, as midwestern Christians we had no real reference point for "chicken fat," which was mentioned about every three pages.

I began to find some of this spirit of irony and to welcome anarchic nonsense in books: Swift, certainly; Mark Twain more than occasionally; more softly in James Thurber and other humorists; H. Allen Smith. Unofficial, very funny, and consciously subversive of social and religious pieties. About this time, Donald Barthelme, a few years older than I, was discovering Ambrose Bierce down in Houston. Judging from the superhero disguise of Raketmensch in *Gravity's Rainbow* and a lot of other evidence in his novels, Thomas Pynchon was discovering *Mad* about the same time. Good Catholic upbringing there too, come to think of it.

More to the point, writers like these two, and John Barth from Maryland, Joseph Heller from New York City, and Alvin Greenberg from Cincinnati, helped a whole generation to escape the dead-end, Europeanized view that Art had to have the kind of desperate, sepia-toned seriousness found in the novels of Saul Bellow and Norman Mailer and Amiri Baraka's "Preface to a Twenty-Volume Suicide Note."

Some years before I saw the first *Mad*, I read a real suicide note. On the premise that everyone needed a hot meal at noon and unable to get me to it herself, my mother had arranged for me to eat dinner at the house of some people who lived near downtown. I never heard of them before or after. They weren't Catholics, I think, and the overfurnished and overheated rooms seemed as strange to me as the food and customs. But what the hell, I was about ten, and I ate the food and kept my mouth shut and my ears and eyes open, acting for a change on my mother's often-repeated advice.

One of the things I heard, in whispers and hints, was that one of the older daughters had tried, in noticeably inefficient fashion, to commit suicide. Furthermore, she had left a long note of explanation, justification, condemnation, whatever. In great stealth and secrecy, one of her younger sisters offered to show it to me as something rare and awe-inspiring. Having been taught that suicide was the ultimate sin, I was prepared to be impressed by the tragedy and grandeur of it all.

We stole up to one of the bedrooms—I have an impression of rather drab and lumpy quilts—and she pulled out a narrow notebook with wide-lined, narrow leaves and handed it to me with a near-flourish.

The text, rambling and formless, drew its sentiments and language from the kind of lumpen-realistic true confession and modern romance magazines I had sneaked away from baby-sitters who thought I was too young to be able to read, let alone understand, such advanced stuff. The notion of someone marching up to the verge of eternal damnation in this kind of language was appalling not just because of the lack of faith and hope but of the lack of style. If art could influence life—and clearly it had in this case—then I decided that in my case the kind of art wasn't going to be realism. That was not only dangerous; it was boring. The problem was finding a style I could live with that didn't imply suicide, liver, or *David Copperfield*.

Home and Away

B y the time I was sixteen, I would cringe when my mother defended Boonville as "a good place to raise kids" because, as far as I could tell, there was nothing to see and not only nothing for me to do but no way for me to imagine doing it. To try to find a place and a role, I had to leave.

There seemed to be a lot of places to go. When I was a child, the cityscapes of movies and novels seemed as remote and alien to me as John Carter's Helium or Dorothy's Oz. Later, even Kansas City and St. Louis, three and four hours' drive away on the two-lane roads, seemed almost as exotic. Our journey was not to the city as geopolitical unit but the city as magical space. The dancers at the Starlight Theater in Kansas City and the future Hall of Famers at Sportsman's Park—sometimes actually playing in the sense of fooling around for amusement during warmup—were as remote from my experience as the giraffes at the zoo were from the Jersey cows I milked.

These experiences provided material for daydream and even for emulation. I wore Duke Snider's number 4 on my uniform, taught myself to bat left-handed, and played center field on a local baseball team, but I knew that my impersonation was implausible, and finally it was absorbed by the reality principle. When I watched musical comedy, I could not even fashion a daydream to put me in the place of the actors, though of course I wanted to live like the characters in a neatly defined world in which true love was gracefully and harmoniously rewarded. Until, years later, I read about Emma Bovary's response to *Lucia di Lammermore*, I did not know that anyone else responded that way to the spectacle glowing in the dark.

For a time—it must have been the summer of 1946—the city took on a new dimension, for I was taken there not as part of a gawking crowd but as a very junior partner on men's business. Periodically—once a week? every two weeks?—Dad would spend a short night in my bed, and I would try to sleep as I clung to the edge of my side of the mattress. We would rise at 2:00 A.M. and ride in the big red International truck with the dull silver box bed to the market in Kansas City to buy fruit and vegetables for his wholesale produce business. The market was another magical space. For one thing, we made so many turns in dark and unfamiliar territory that the sun seemed to rise in the north. For another, the market was filled with swarthy Mediterranean types, speaking in clipped and hurried speech, very different from the solid, stolid, drawling German-Americans who inhabited Cooper County. But they were not on a stage or a baseball field; they were all round me, ignoring me as if I were one of what still seems to me a cast of characters.

Best of all, Dad turned me loose, with pocket change, to buy my own breakfast at a restaurant full of grown-ups getting ready to go to work. I can't quite remember what I ordered—it wasn't anything I ate on a normal day, but I always got the same thing and consumed it, trying not to watch the people too closely or otherwise look too much out of place. Good practice for later meals in more conventionally exotic places.

Then I would walk to join Dad past heaped-up produce, some of it in colors and smells strange to a child raised on meat, potatoes, over-boiled green beans, and cole slaw suspended in green Jell-o, past men waving hands holding stubby, wickedly curved knives. The men looked alive and unaccountable, even dangerous, doing things I could not even begin to understand, in streets packed and littered as nothing in Boonville ever was. I never got lost, but there was a thrill in the notion that I could get lost and considerable satisfaction in the fact that I never did.

I never brought anything back to Boonville, except once a hot pepper that I fed to my younger brother and got beaten for, and I don't remember coming back. Probably I was tired from the early hours and the imaginative excitement. No doubt I was resisting the return to reality.

In recent years, I have disappointed friends kind enough to give me tours because I have looked at their local markets—in Paris, Budapest, Saint John, Philadelphia—and been unable to feign the expected surprise or delight. None are as exotic as the market in Kansas City fixed by the memory of a skinny eleven-year-old.

Five years after these trips to market I was a very callow Rockhurst College freshman actually living in Kansas City, able and indeed compelled to explore, to find my way around. I still had trouble orienting myself downtown—I would come out of one of the gilded, three-tiered movie theaters unable to decide which way to go to reach the streetcar stop, sometimes having to walk around the block to discover which way was north. But within a few months I was giving directions to the natives (many of whom seemed curiously incurious about their environment), had mastered the complex grid of bus and streetcar lines, had learned not to start at a panhandler's pitch or at the sight of black people dominating a street by style and by numbers, and had become able to pass, if it was not too close to election time, the unspoken and unofficial tests administered by bartenders.

I was also learning to deal with differences in language and in time. Set amid a group of supercilious and odd-sounding students from St. Louis, my mid-Missouri drawl was quickened, my vowels sharpened and differentiated. In the art cinemas I saw worlds less glittering but more compelling than those of the Hollywood movies I had seen at the Lyric, and the characters talked and acted even in ways that by comparison made the people in the market (to which I had not, never have, returned) seem like people in downtown Boonville.

Even the Kansas City *Star*, which I had read for ten years and which seemed the largest newspaper anyone could imagine, was different. I discovered, with astonishment and delight, that one could buy the Sunday edition of the *Star* on Saturday night. So Kansas City was at least a day ahead of Boonville. And since there were people moving around all the time and doing new and different things, the Sunday morning edition had to be different from the Saturday night Sunday edition.

More important, though there were always people around, it was possible to be alone. In Boonville, it was almost impossible to be alone because everyone seemed to know me. It was possible to be lonely because there was nothing new to look at, nothing to try to understand because it was already, always had been, just there, nothing to take you out of yourself or show you that there were other possibilities, other roles, some pleasant, some not. Even in Kansas City, at seventeen through twenty, expeditions with my friends often seemed foolish and pointless, generating a false hilarity that must have annoyed the citizenry and that embarrasses me almost forty years later. When I was on a date, I sometimes felt as if I were imitating a grown-up and about to be exposed.

But alone, coming home from a date or just wandering, I was satisfied by the melancholy of solitude, in the crowd but not of it, able to see the fringes of other lives without having to touch or unravel them, anonymous and separate from church or family or any social tie. Through the window of the Troost Avenue streetcar I could safely view rib joints and tamale carts and storefront churches like the Sweet Hour of Prayer Spiritual Temple and then arrive at the major downtown stores with

rack on rack of unaffordable merchandise and display windows arranged with a style that made them more than quantitatively different
from Sunnyday's and Glover's on Main Street in Boonville. And the
sleazy hotels ("Room 25 cents. With Electric Light 30 cents") and bars
and burlesque theater and the live music—rhythm and blues and saxo-
phones dominated—told me that there was a whole way of life that
Chestnut Street at home, with a liquor store and a pool hall, both
rather tacky, on opposite sides of Main Street, had only intimated as a
possibility for people who didn't care about respectability. Although I
enjoyed the music, I was not really drawn to this kind of life; I was still,
occasionally, an altar boy, a good, respectable boy who perhaps read too
much and had an odd view of the social pieties that my parents tried
to believe in or anyhow inculcate. But the sleaze in Kansas City, I now
see, echoed something in my subconscious and in the subconscious of
the whole region. The dangerous and desirable things did not have to
be beautiful—better, to my smalltown sensibilities, that they not be—
but it was right and necessary, fitting indeed and just, for them to be.
And for me to be amid them if not in them or of them.

I began to see roles that I could admire without hoping to emulate.
Jay McShann, in the fifties not an institution but simply leader of a
seven-piece group playing the small clubs along Troost Avenue, seemed
heroic in an understated fashion, not because of his music, which I listened to as often as the bartender didn't throw me out, but because of
his ability to keep going after the collapse of his big band and the tragic
death of Charlie Parker. Because of a vestigial romanticism, I never
quite doubted the scrawls maintaining "Bird Lives," but Jay McShann
didn't even have to show me that he was alive; he just put on a show.

Of course, though I too was alive, or so I hoped, I was not really living
in Kansas City: as a student, I was just passing through on my way to
somewhere else, and though I had a number of sensations, I had no

sense of pattern in the people and very little in the physical setting. For the next seven years I was, as a graduate student, in a situation where there was only one role, that of the scholar, and the only question was, and to some extent still is, whether I could fill that role. About the time it seemed that I might be able to, I moved to Chicago and, though I did not abandon the library, felt as though I had emerged from a cave. Everything about the city and my response to it seemed new. It was not so much my technical status as grown-up, voter, married man with a full-time job and something like a real income but that I was approaching a city as a place of pattern, to be studied as well as perceived as magic space. For one thing, I had a map, so that I could see that the city had not just happened, it had been planned, and even the accidents and anomalies of human history had been incorporated in that plan. Streets to the north, avenues to the south; everything east-west, north-south, except for Milwaukee and Ogden and the other angled avenues and later the freeways, which imposed an almost symmetrical pattern over the basic grid.

The texture of Chicago was a good deal more complex and harder to read than the pattern. The neighborhoods were more various; the streets more colorful. Sometimes literally, like West Madison Street, where the inhabitants shaded, almost block by block, from grubby white derelict to deep black to brown to white again and finally, on the far west side, to pink in the flamingos on the patches of lower middle-class lawns. The languages were multiplied and bewildering. I could track across the FM dial and hear languages I could not even identify, and in some districts even the signs were not translated for outsiders. If you wanted a lawyer, you didn't belong on Milwaukee Avenue; there you could only get an Awocat.

And you didn't have to be from Boonville to be an outsider. Neighborhoods outside one's own were really foreign, not just in space but in language and atmosphere, the food in the restaurants and the goods in the stores. This had probably been true in Kansas City, but the contrast in Chicago, like that between the north shore and the projects where I dared not walk and felt uncomfortable even riding past, was sharp enough for me to learn to see it. A ride on the El and subway from the Loyola stop to the end of the line on the south side gave me a sense of economic and political reality as all the classes in American citizenship and the college courses in intellectual history could not have done.

Besides, Chicago had dimension as well as structure and texture. Kansas City had tall buildings, but not, in the early 1950s, enough of them to constitute a real skyline, and though it obviously had what we now call an infrastructure and what even then we called an underworld, it had no underground in the British sense. My first ride on the El produced a new kind of assault on all my senses: looking down into graveyards and into second-story windows, smelling and tasting the soot that blew in the open windows, sticking to the plastic seats, and being deafened by the roar when the train dived into the tunnel and became a subway. Hell must be like this, I thought, but I could see that the other riders did not seem to think so, or if they did, they gave no sign. As I too got used to it, I revised my definition of cities to exclude those which had no subways, and this held until I saw cities, some of them tiny by Chicago standards, which were founded in the Middle Ages.

But Chicago and other American cities with subways have one thing in common with medieval cities because they are, by sections at least, designed for the pedestrian. In Kansas City I had often walked, by necessity, but in Chicago it was possible to stroll. Old Town, with its remodeled houses, brightly painted doors, and exterior decor suggesting artistic sensibility within (one house sported a horse-holding jockey with the features painted white, the ultimate white liberal variant on Flannery O'Connor's "The Artificial Nigger"), made a claim that the city could be civil as well as civic. The hospital and office district southeast of the Water Tower, deserted on a Saturday morning and brushed clean by the wind off the lake, seemed like part of my marvelous, re-current dream in which I find unsuspected rooms in a familiar house.

As I began to live into Chicago, each new neighborhood came to seem both strange and familiar. However alien the ethnic or linguis-tic group was, I came to see that all had the same basic needs: food, communications, sources of money, clothes, health or police protec-tion, escape from health and police protection, education, edification. And when I understood that, I could still feel lonely or alienated or frightened or insecure—most rarely when I was alone—but I could never really be lost. A map became not just a scheme of lines but an aesthetic pattern, a guide to financial and political and demographic arrangements.

So Kansas City had shown me the magic of cities, but Chicago taught me how to read a city and to get a sense of the life around me, not as I might imagine myself in it or as it affected me, but just as being there, for and in itself rather than being something for me to contemplate. While in any new city I am still an outsider, I could never quite be just a tourist again.

But I still had to discover that to know a city, you have not only to walk it but sit in it. This is something I could not learn in Boonville or Kansas City or even Chicago, perhaps because I was impressed by the pace of the city-dwellers and had no sense that it was possible to sit. But as I grew older and visited cities less bustling than Chicago, I real-ized that urbanites do far better at enjoying their space than people in small towns. In fact, space in small towns is not really defined or used; it is just there. A French friend remarked that these towns seemed sad because one never saw any people in them, and while this is an exag-geration, Americans at least do not seem to use space as city-dwellers do. For one thing, smalltown Americans don't walk unless they abso-lutely have to; for another, there is no place for them to stop when they do walk; for a third, there isn't anything much to look at when they do stop. The best cities provide parks and benches for their citizens, not just in the public squares or in historic spots like the Arènes de Lutece but just scattered about. Small towns have parks, but people tend to go there to do something—play baseball or have picnics or let the children swing. The only green space in downtown Boonville, and that at the Missouri River end of Main Street, is the courthouse lawn, and when I was a boy only elderly blacks ever sat on the retaining wall—there were no benches—that surrounded it, and they had nothing to look at but the storefronts opposite. Not more than three blocks away, a park overlooks the river. In all the years I lived in Boonville I never saw anyone in it. But in cities, which are supposed to be full of harried people, I saw people just sitting, perhaps reading or writing a letter or something like a draft of this chapter. One of the many marvelous things in Manhattan is a small park in Midtown, the width of a building, with benches, some potted greenery, and a sheet of water cascading down a wall of pebbles set in concrete. This little space was financed privately in memory of someone whose name I do not recall but whose legacy is unforgettable.

The habit of sitting or strolling or just hanging out affects everything one sees, even the grand vistas and monuments of the postcards. Monet was right: you have not seen anything if you see it only once. Like Monet's cathedral at Rouen, Notre Dame changes every hour, and the Seine or Danube cannot be known from a single point.

Moreover, the leisured living into a city affects everything: the patterns of movement and stares of the people; the blending or contrast of the styles and materials of the buildings; the vistas that open before one—not just in the starred or rayed areas of the guidebooks. The grandeur of a city is in these sights, and in the years of my middle-aged version of the Grand Tour, taken not as preparation for adult life but as compensation for it, I sought out most of them.

But I came to feel that the charm of a city is not in these or in any magical place like the Louvre or the Uffizi or San Marco but in sights and buildings not noted that tell as much about the society as the major monuments tell about the past. Even Florence and Venice have churches that are not baroque or gothic, that contain no major or even minor works of art, and that testify to the real contemporary culture of the people. The Italians feel something of this: the ex-votos and candles surround not the paintings by Fra Lippo Lippi or Tintoretto (just as well, because of the heat and smoke) but statues and paintings of more recent date and less obvious—or no—aesthetic interest.

Even the monstrous can come to have a certain appeal. The building at the corner of Tanács Körút and Bajcsy-Zsilinszky Street in downtown Pest must be a mixture of a half-dozen styles, including classical and Turkish, and its color seems to Western eyes (the Hungarians seem to favor it for churches) a horrible mud-mustard off-yellow. No photograph, even one taken with a wide-angle lens, can do it justice: it extends around two corners. At first I thought it the ugliest building in Europe, if not the whole world, but as I passed it every day for three months, I came to see it as a digest of turn-of-the-century Hungarian architecture and have friendly and nostalgic feelings for it.

As I came to recognize that, even to the natives, the past, however glorious, is past, that people actually live in these places, I began to search out evidence of the common life which in a perverse way seems more exotic in Venice or Marseilles than it did in Boonville. The vistas into the courtyards of blocks of twentieth-century flats in downtown Pest came to seem more picturesque and mysterious than the ancient courtyards on Castle Hill in Buda. The awe at the idea of living in a city waned, but there was still a sense of mystery in people so immersed in their lives that they could ignore the ruin of a Roman arena or use it for soccer games as if it were an ordinary park.

In fact, even the most glorious city can be lonely if there is not some sign that it is—and was—inhabited by human beings as unaccountable and idiosyncratic as I like to think myself. My sharpest and most personal memories, snapshots in my personal album, come from evidence that magical and human space can overlap: a soccer ball floating in the Grand Canal at dawn under a sky cut in half by a cloud bank over the Adriatic; a man carrying a hooded hawk in the Deák Tér metro station in Budapest; three Asians at the top of the flight of steps from Sacre Cour singing, in English, "I Want to Hold Your Hand"; trading jazz tune lines about red beans and rice with a group of metro musicians in an Antillean restaurant; Johnny Cash's voice coming from an eighteenth-century window in the Castle district of Budapest; the old men playing a version of boccie across the Roman arena from boys playing soccer; a cat almost catching a pigeon in the Musée de Cluny; Parisians reacting to the hydraulic-lift, power-brush motorcycles of the dog-shit patrol; graffiti carved by Renaissance workmen on the back of an unfinished Michelangelo statue; a Madonna in Venice with brown hair and braids and a fully clothed St. Sebastian in Florence; really feeling, in the signs and records of revolutionary iconoclasm, the astonishing energy in and depth of the hatred for the church and the monarchy; turning on the radio just after arriving in Paris to stay at a hotel where Jean-Paul Sartre lived and hearing Elmore James singing the old blues song, "It Hurts Me Too."

One day in the Louvre I caught up with a tour group of Missouri farmers. They didn't look like family, but they looked very familiar. None was from Boonville—I asked—though one had a sister living there, and none actually knew my father, though some knew of him. Seeing them made me feel further from Boonville than ever and more at home where I was.

But of course I was not really at home. As a tourist inventorying monuments or a traveler (the distinction made by Paul Fussell in *Abroad* is probably not original) encountering the life of the city more deeply, I am an alien, unable, whatever the local language, to talk to the natives except in the most superficial manner. Jake Barnes speaks the language like a native in *The Sun Also Rises*, but he is not a native, and the dialogue reveals it—whether Hemingway knows it or not, and it is healthy not to make that mistake. Sometimes I was lonely; I felt happiest when working, alone, in a strange place because seated at a desk I was locked into what had become a comfortable role and walking outside I didn't have to worry about not playing other roles adequately. The real loneliness could be deflected or deferred by the encounter with another culture, by the thrill of dislocation, by seeing—through bifocals, as it turned out—a world in which I am still that ingenu riding to Kansas City or St. Louis for the first time.

In fact, after I stopped trying to imagine myself in a role away from Boonville, I began to see it more clearly. Looking at the Danube, I remembered the Missouri, and the double vision helped me to understand the rivers and the people who lived along them in a different way. Seeing the Missouri farmers in the Louvre, I understood the French Revolution better and the strength of my own region. And I began to see myself, as person and writer, in a new way as I thought about where I had come from and where I had gone. It took me six years to get the farmers into a poem because it took that long to get myself out of the way.

Oddly, when I stopped thinking about a role, people began to cast me. A third party told me that someone who had heard me give a formal talk and then declaim in Grandpa Murray's free-style fashion said, "He's a smart son of a bitch. But he *is* smart." A quintessentially New York friend is unshakably convinced that she first saw me in lizard-skin cowboy boots and Stetson, neither of which I have ever possessed.

Another urged me to buy a leather poncho and then, maybe, get a flat-crowned hat and a cigarillo. A friend of my daughter thought I looked like Clint Eastwood. Yes, I answered, we're both getting bald and kind of stringy-looking. I can't be John Wayne any more than I can be Duke Snider, though it gives me a belated sense of satisfaction and surprise when someone seems to think I can. Even more surprising was the remark of a very bright student that he liked my class because I was always so cheerful. So I still don't have my father's looks, at least from the neck up, or his character.

I have begun to realize that, wherever I go, I always leave from Boonville as the skinny, uncertain teenager, and that the Davises and Murrays are the real audience I play to, the family albums the ones I look at more than the ones I compiled. Over the years I have gone back to Boonville many times. At first my parents worried about my character. Mom was concerned that I didn't suffer fools gladly, which was funny considering her character. Dad gave me a pamphlet called *Tact*, which was even funnier considering his, and worried that people in Boonville would think me weird because I carried two different brands of cigarettes. Mom didn't live to see me as an adult character in the family saga, and perhaps she couldn't have lived long enough. Dad plays a larger part than she in this book because he lived to see me find my role and to acknowledge that it was suitable. He came to believe, wrongly, that I could be rude to anyone I wanted and get away with it, and he seemed to take a good deal of satisfaction in this view.

The survivors in the extended family seem less interested in the quality of my character than in the fact that I seem to live in a picaresque novel and, except for Cary and perhaps my baby sister, on whom ten years' start seems barely enough, the most eccentric in the story. My nephew Matt, who does look and act and talk very much like my father, gave as a mock excuse for swearing the precedent of his Uncle

Bob. (My father, hearing this, said, "Well, Bob, you *do* cuss too damn much." He was perfectly serious.) My brother, who turned out to look more like the real Uncle Bob than Dad from the neck down, tells old stories to the next generation and finds new ones to embellish from the often prosaic facts. My daughter says that, when she talks about me to her friends, they say, "I wish I had him for a father."

Whatever part I play in the story, though, when I return to Boonville I am neither tourist nor citizen, literally disoriented because north seems east to me. I can't say that I have paid a price for leaving because I know—have known for forty years—that leaving was the only possible choice.

When my father was lying in the hospital, I sat under the walnut trees in his yard after my daughter left, looking out over the stretch of the lawn, for what seemed like the last time, with a melancholy acceptance. In fact, I have gone back, even when I wasn't on my way somewhere else. The family did not end when he died or when Grandpa's son, the only male child from the family in that generation, died without issue. I can go home again, but home has for a long time been a magic space, surrounded by but not in a Boonville that is both familiar and strange, to be experienced briefly and rarely, never to be inhabited, and always present in imagination.

Robert Murray Davis is a professor of English at the University of Oklahoma. His books include *Brideshead Revisited: The Past Redeemed*, *Evelyn Waugh and the Forms of His Time*, and *Outside the Lines*, a poetry collection.